Witnesses

to the One

Witnesses to the One

THE SPIRITUAL HISTORY OF THE SH'MA

Rabbi Joseph B. Meszler

Foreword by Rabbi Elyse Goldstein

JEWISH LIGHTS Publishing

Woodstock, Vermont

Witnesses to the One:
The Spiritual History of the Sh'ma

2006 First Printing
© 2006 by Joseph B. Meszler

Library of Congress Cataloging-in-Publication Data
Meszler, Joseph B.
Witnesses to the One : the spiritual history of the Sh'ma / Joseph B. Meszler ; foreword by Elyse Goldstein.
    p. cm.
Includes bibliographical references.
ISBN-13: 978-1-58023-309-5 (hardcover)
ISBN-10: 1-58023-309-0 (hardcover)
1. Shema. 2. God (Judaism) 3. Spiritual life–Judaism. I. Title.
BM670.S45M47 2006
296.4'5–dc22

2006015174

10   9   8   7   6   5   4   3   2   1

Manufactured in the United States of America
Jacket Design: Tim Holtz

Published by Jewish Lights Publishing
A Division of Longhill Partners, Inc.
Sunset Farm Offices, Route 4, P. O. Box 237
Woodstock, VT 05091
Tel: (802) 457-4000   Fax: (802) 457-4004
www.jewishlights.com

Contents

Foreword

Sh'ma—to hear, to listen, to understand. I've said it myself every night before going to bed since I was a little girl. In those days it was comforting, quieting. It meant someone was looking out for me, even if I thought that someone was a Divine Old Man with a beard on a throne in heaven.

As I grew up those familiar words became a struggle for my feminist consciousness. The Old Man was no longer relevant; worse, I was angry at Him for His masculine standards that cast me aside as an Other. If He existed at all, He surely wasn't looking down on me, a rebellious teenager who dared to question the status quo for Jewish women.

But I missed the soft feeling of the words of the *Sh'ma*, so I went back to look again. I started to understand that the words signaled not a dogma or a creed, but a process and a journey. On that journey, I could understand the Oneness of everything, both Divine and human. I could listen to the ancient melodies with a new spirit. I could hear the call of the *Sh'ma* as a call to social action leading to the ultimate improvement of the world—a call for both women and men. I see the *Sh'ma* now not as a doxology of faith in the Old Man, but as a dialogue with the Divine in all the forms It takes and however It calls back to us.

As an adult the power of the *Sh'ma* has never left me, but when I chose to make outreach my life's work as a rabbi I came to another place of reconciliation with the *Sh'ma*. I've been working

long enough with unaffiliated, marginalized Jews to know that not
everyone resonates with this simplest of Jewish prayers. They
haven't heard it, they aren't listening, and they don't understand.
It still surprises me, but it no longer shocks me, that there are Jews
who never said a bedtime *Sh'ma*, that it wasn't the first prayer they
learned in religious school (because they never went to one), that
they can't imagine saying it on their deathbeds. For them, the
Sh'ma holds no historic associations; its mystical beauty is uninter-
esting, its lyrical, simple meaning worlds away from their daily lives.
For me, the *Sh'ma* is poetry; for them, it is only words, words they
don't know or care about or feel in their souls. It is hard for most
affiliated Jews to understand this. The *Sh'ma* seems the "bottom
line" that, at the very least, every Jew knows and loves. Welcome to
the world of Jewish outreach, to the discovery that even the *Sh'ma*
in English is foreign to many.

That is why this book is so precious, for it will open a new
pathway of communication for so many. Its dialogue with Jewish
prayer only begins with the *Sh'ma*, but moves on to the great philosophical questions of a Jewish life: Why bother being Jewish at all?
What can modern Judaism do with its roots? Can the teachers and
thinkers of the past illuminate this complicated life we lead now?

I think they can, and I think this book will help those teachers reach out across the generations to grab hold of the person
who feels adrift, who is bored by conventional answers, who rejects
platitudes but still feels the desire to be "in" this rich heritage. We
should be grateful to Joseph Meszler for starting this conversation.

So, to Jews who are moved by social action and *tikkun olam*,
the *Sh'ma* says: be an iconoclast as Moses was; stand in protest as
Akiba did; speak the polemic as Saadia spoke; let the *Sh'ma* call you
to action as Heschel was called. To Jews who fear being swallowed
by the community, the *Sh'ma* says: affirm your uniqueness even in
the face of a community as Maimonides did. To Jews who are
attracted to a mystical realm, the *Sh'ma* says: try to unify all realms,
especially the male and female ones, as Kabbalah and Luria tried;
reach for the Messiah, as Luzzatto reached. To the unaffiliated

Jewish people who shake their heads at the internal fractiousness of the denominations, the *Sh'ma* says: we are all unified even if we don't act it, as Kook felt. And to those who feel Judaism does not answer them when they call, let the *Sh'ma* leave its imprint, as it did on Baeck, when it says: you are not alone.

Perhaps the *Sh'ma* as a "mantra" of all these facets can be the door leading them back in. And for those of us already in, it is time to renew and rediscover that what we knew as children holds great intellectual depth for us as adults. As it says in the Talmud *"ta Sh'ma"*—come, learn, and hear. For some, it will be hearing for the first time and for others *as if* for the first time—but for everyone, this book is a call.

Rabbi Elyse Goldstein

Preface

Sh'ma Yisrael Adonai Eloheinu Adonai echad. "Hear O Israel, the Eternal is our God, the Eternal is One!" (Deuteronomy 6:4).[1]

There is no more important statement in Judaism than the *Sh'ma*. Whenever Jews recite or sing these words it is an important moment. If Judaism originated monotheism, the belief in one God, then the *Sh'ma* is the embodiment of this world-changing idea. It is a proclamation and a command, yet people recite it like a prayer. There is even a long tradition of reciting these words when one rises in the morning and before going to bed at night. Many Jewish parents sing these words to their children before they go to sleep.

My daughter, who is almost three years old, already knows these words. We have been singing them to her at bedtime since the first day of her life. When she says them, I feel a sense of awe at her ability to learn, but more than that I feel I am transmitting something sacred.

My son is another matter. At the time of this writing, he is only one and a half years old, and I have no expectation that he should be able to recite a Hebrew prayer. He only knows a few words, like "up" and "down." For most of his life he has had fluid in his ears that has affected his hearing and speech development. The doctors reassure me that he will undergo a very simple, noninvasive surgery to correct the problem, yet for the moment he hears everything as if he were underwater and probably has since birth. He cannot enunciate very much at all. While I know this will pass, I wonder what these words at bedtime sound like to him.

The first two words of the *Sh'ma* are usually translated as "Hear O Israel." The "O" is vocative. Hear. Listen. Pay attention. Early childhood specialists tell us that some 50 percent of our brain development occurs before the age of five.[2] Are these words somehow being impressed upon the makeup of his being? As I hold him in the glider at night, as he clings to his worn teddy bear and closes his eyes, I gently rock him. It is my favorite time of day. Bedtime is the time when I feel most prayerful. I imagine that I am not alone in this feeling, for the idea of "bedtime prayers" occurs in many religions all over the world. There is something about putting a child to sleep, about reflecting on the day that has passed, about holding a life in my arms that moves me from a place so deep inside I can only call it primordial. So I sing the ancient words of the *Sh'ma* into my son's water-filled ears.

The words of the *Sh'ma* can be translated in a variety of ways. One complication for translation into English is that there is no present tense of the verb "to be" in biblical Hebrew. Any English translation has to use the word "is," which does not have a direct correlation to the Hebrew.

In addition, the *Sh'ma* contains the Name of God twice, spelled with the Hebrew letters *yod-heh-vav-heh.* No one knows how to pronounce this name, so Jews as an act of piety substitute the title Adonai during prayer, which means "Lord." Others attempt to translate this name into English as best they can, most commonly "Eternal." I like to represent it with equivalent English letters in a way similar to how it appears in Hebrew: YHVH.

This leads us to the most literal translation of the *Sh'ma*: "Hear O Israel YHVH our God YHVH one."

The meaning of the *Sh'ma* is admittedly ambiguous. Why "hear"? Why not "see" or "look"? What does the Name of God signify? Where do we put an "is"? What does the Torah mean by "one" after all? What does it really mean to believe in one God?

Despite this ambiguity, the words of the *Sh'ma* are among the first Hebrew words Jewish children learn. Jews have closed their eyes and meditated on them for centuries. Converts to Judaism memorize them. We know that people have died for these words, even been martyred for what they represent. Clearly, this is a statement that holds great power.

Yet too many members of the Jewish community simply recite the *Sh'ma* without feeling the force behind its words. They come to the synagogue prayer service too often uninspired, unmoved. The synagogue service fails them. They recite the *Sh'ma*, mechanically mouthing the syllables. The sound fills the sanctuary, but many of the people Israel do not (or cannot) hear. Either they are emotionally numb because they are reciting the *Sh'ma* by rote or they simply lack understanding. They have a different kind of obstacle to their hearing than my son.

The hearing of the *Sh'ma* demands a different kind of listening, one that is not meant to be passed on unthinkingly. As much as Judaism is often described as a religion of "deed, not creed," the *Sh'ma* points to a belief that we are compelled to explore. We are supposed to hear something more than just its sound.

We all know that there are many different kinds of listening that we can do. Sometimes we "half-listen." We tune out and then perk up when our name is called. Other times we listen just to glean what we need, such as when we call "Information" for a telephone number. Or we take in the sounds of music or of nature, listening to birds at a bird feeder or the sudden silence of snow.

There are the rare times when face-to-face with someone that we truly listen. We listen to the voice's inflection and see the emotions on the face. We are fully present in our listening, and we pay attention to the smallest detail. We can repeat back to the other exactly what he or she has said, and we feel connected, bonded, even vulnerable.

In a similar fashion, when the people of Israel received the Ten Commandments at Mount Sinai, they said, *Na'aseh v'nishma*, "We will do and we will hear" (Exodus 24:7).

Normally we have to hear the instructions for something before we do something. Before we follow an order, we have to know what is expected of us. When people come to us and request, "Do me a favor," we want to know what they are asking.

But the Israelites said that first they would do and then they would hear. Clearly they meant something different than common listening, the taking in of information, when they said they would hear. It seems to have more to do with understanding. We will do the commandments, and as a result, we will hear what we were meant to understand through their doing. Some things we only understand after we experience them. Sometimes we learn through trying something out. Hearing follows the doing. It seems to be closer to the older English word "hearken."

It may not seem natural to us to think of hearing as a primary form of understanding. People seem more inclined to visualization in Western culture. We use phrases like "seeing is believing" and "picture this." A schoolteacher once demonstrated for me that if you tell a class to touch their ears while standing in front of them and touching your nose, they will inevitably all touch their noses, following the visual cue over the auditory. In addition, the English words "theory" and "idea" originate in the idea of sight; "theory" comes from the Greek *theoria*, which means "to look at," and "idea" comes from *idein*, which means "to see."[3] In contrast, a contemporary Hebrew expression used when we want someone to pay attention is *tishma*, "hear," which is a command to listen more closely. A similar expression used frequently in the Babylonian Talmud to make a point in an argument is *ta sh'ma*, "come and hear."[4] In other words, it may seem more natural for Western thinkers to grasp an idea with our sight, and it may take more of an effort to truly listen. Nevertheless, this is precisely the effort that the *Sh'ma* asks of us. In Jewish tradition, hearing is believing.

The *Sh'ma* seems to be commanding us to hear in a profound way. It seems to be saying: Pay attention. Listen. Understand.

Reflect. Be ready to act on what you hear. Be ready to be transformed. The true hearer perceives the currents that flow underneath the words, the tides of history that have given these words
meaning. This kind of hearing is active.

The *Sh'ma* does more than defy direct translation. It has also
meant different things throughout history. Different Jews have
meant different things at different times when they recited these
words. While they all meant, in some underlying sense, belief in
one God, that belief took on different colors and nuances,
depending upon the pushes and pulls of the era. What Moses
meant was different than what the Sages of antiquity meant, which
in turn was different than the philosophers, than the mystics, and
so on. Like light shimmering through water, how we hear the
Sh'ma depends on refractions of time and place.

The primary purpose of this book is to investigate the spiritual history of the *Sh'ma* and to hopefully inspire the seeker to find
meaning in these famous words. We will try to literally heed the
command to "hear." We will hear not only the words but also the
stories of the important people who have uttered them in generations past. Meeting these figures along the way is the second purpose of this work. Understanding the lives of past thinkers is a
necessary step in the history of monotheism, and we will join them
in the search for meaning. They are witnesses to the One. We can
guess how they might have translated the words of the *Sh'ma,* what
it meant to them, and what it might mean to us. Every generation
has found a different dimension of truth in pursuing the One, and
this search continues with us. If we have truly heard, perhaps we
will feel compelled to do something significant in response. The
same way sound has to penetrate and echo through the fluid in my
son's ears, so does the *Sh'ma* come, sometimes distorted, but nevertheless real, down to us, containing something sacred.

Each chapter begins with a different translation of the *Sh'ma*
depending upon the beliefs of the people presented there. Each
chapter also starts with a story, a fictional re-creation of a historical

moment as we try to enter the minds and lives of these Jewish thinkers. We do so with empathy. We are then introduced to their thought, never straying too far from the implications of the *Sh'ma* as our theme. Each time we must ask ourselves, what does it mean not only to hear the *Sh'ma* but to hear this person from that time and place? A discussion guide is available to help with this endeavor.

If we can find the witnesses' perspective of the central truth contained within the *Sh'ma*, then the story may become sacred to us. It is sacred if it becomes a part of our personal story. It is true if we relive their stories in some fashion and see them in human experience today.

I wonder what my children will understand as they grow and learn these six Hebrew words. On a deeper level than his fluid-filled ears can absorb, I pray that my son is able to take in the many meanings that these words contain beyond physically just hearing them, that they penetrate his heart. I imagine that only through a great amount of doing, of life experience, will the words of the *Sh'ma* reach both of my children in their souls. I pray that they continue to reach me and others as well.

A Note on Translations

For translations of the Bible, I have relied heavily upon the *JPS Hebrew-English Tanakh* (Philadelphia: Jewish Publication Society of America, 1999), yet I have tried when possible to adapt the translation so that God appears beyond gender, using W. Gunther Plaut, ed., *The Torah: A Modern Commentary,* revised edition (New York: URJ Press, 2005) as my guide. I have also deviated from the JPS translation when I felt the context called for it. All translations of Rabbinic texts are my own. Regularly I paraphrased certain texts to make them accessible to a reader new to this literature. Readers are welcome to look in the notes for references. In quotations of other works, however, I have let the masculine gender bias remain in order to present each thinker with integrity.

Acknowledgments

I would like to thank Stuart M. Matlins, publisher, and everyone at Jewish Lights Publishing for bringing this moment of inspiration to the public. Thank you to the congregants of Temple Sinai of Sharon, Massachusetts, and Washington Hebrew Congregation in Washington, D.C., for the discussions that generated these chapters. I would like to thank David Vise for his friendship, for his leadership in the Jewish community, and for setting in motion the publishing of this book. I would also like to thank those who read the manuscript or otherwise made innumerable suggestions: Gerdy Trachtman, David Bachrach, Rabbi Barry Kogan, Rabbi Gustav Buchdahl, and my sister, Joelle Reizes.

Most of all, I would like to dedicate this book to my wife, Rabbi Julie Zupan, who is my teacher as well as the love of my life.

שמע ישראל

Hear O Israel,

יי אלהינו

YHVH is our God,

יי אחד

YHVH alone!

1
Fighting Idolatry

Moses

A Sacred Story

Moses stood before the Israelites. He looked at them as he spoke, one of the last speeches he would give before he died. He was older than he felt, but the people before him seemed so young. At least they were younger than he. This was not the generation that was raised in slavery in Egypt. This was the generation of their children. They grew up in the wilderness. These Children of Israel were prepared to fight for a land of their own, to follow their God into battle.

But would they remember the covenant, the sacred promises between God and the people Israel? This generation may not have known slavery, but neither had they known the splitting of the Sea of Reeds or the thunder of Mount Sinai. They had not witnessed any plagues, nor had they heard the voice of God declare ten great utterances. They were about to go to war, but would they be faithful?

> You stand this day, all of you, before YHVH your God—your tribal heads, your elders and your officials, all the men of Israel, your children, your wives, even the stranger within your camp, from woodchopper to water drawer—to enter into the covenant of YHVH your God, which YHVH your God is concluding with you this day, with its sanctions. (Deuteronomy 29:9–11)

1

For the people Israel, there could be the worship of only one power, one God for one people. Moses's statement, his last words that make up the end of the Torah, was a demand for loyalty. God had sent different manifestations of the divine to them: plagues in Egypt, the law at Mount Sinai, a pillar of fire and smoke to guide them through the wilderness. All of these different visions came from the same God and bound the people together for the single purpose of forming a covenant. YHVH would be their God, and the people would worship YHVH and no other. The sanctions of the covenant would be severe for those whose hearts betrayed the love of YHVH, but the blessings would be infinitely greater for those who were loyal.

> Hear O Israel, YHVH is our God, YHVH alone! You shall love YHVH with all your heart, with all your soul, and with all your might. (Deuteronomy 6:4–5)

What did Moses mean, in his last great testimony, that the people of Israel were to worship YHVH alone?[1]

"Alone"

The story of the Jewish view of monotheism begins in a time when polytheism, the belief in many gods, was the norm. The Egyptians had a pantheon of gods and goddesses, as did the Canaanites, Phoenicians, Assyrians, and all of the peoples who surrounded the Israelites in the ancient Near East. When Moses introduced YHVH to the people Israel, it began a revolution in thought and belief. Unlike all other deities, YHVH had an unpronounceable name, could not be depicted in an image, and would not tolerate any other god alongside. This revolution, however, was a gradual one, taking centuries to become concretized in the hearts and souls of the people.

The last word of the *Sh'ma* is normally translated as "one," but this is not what Moses meant when he spoke to the Israelites. He was not, in this speech, making a speculative statement about the reality of the universe. Instead, he was making a claim to the people's loyalty. Moses was concerned that the Israelites would disobey God's commandments and break the covenant. The last word of the *Sh'ma, echad,* is therefore best understood as "alone," as in, this is the singular and exclusive Power that you may worship and obey.[2]

There is ambiguity as to whether Moses believed that other gods existed or that YHVH was the only God in nature and history. Moses nowhere denied the existence of other deities but only demanded loyalty to one. The closest hint we have comes from Moses's rhetorical question, "Who is like You, YHVH, among the gods that are worshiped?" (Exodus 15:11). Does this mean that no other gods are like YHVH because they do not exist, at least for the people Israel? Or, more likely, does it mean that YHVH is the greatest God among all of the gods of all the peoples?

In either case, for the ancient Israelite, there could be only one God for the people as a whole and for the individual. Like a general marshaling his troops before going into war, Moses demanded that the people obey their God's orders before they charged into the land of Canaan. They were about to establish themselves in the land of their ancestors and to finally have the security of a real home. Victory would be theirs so long as they stayed faithful to the covenant.

This covenant had taken a generation to solidify. In Egypt and the wilderness, YHVH had to respond to the fear the Israelites felt as they escaped slavery and traveled through treacherous territory. If the people were disloyal, it was because they sought the security of anything they thought might protect them or meet their needs for survival. When the Israelites turned to a golden calf in the wilderness of Sinai, for instance, it was out of a sense of abandonment. Moses had gone up on Mount Sinai to be with God and had been gone long enough that they thought him dead. They felt vulnerable. The people needed a God of might.

This vision of God they received. YHVH went to war on their behalf. As they fought for their survival, they learned through victory that the God of Israel was the strongest. The chieftains of the book of Judges led the way in their settlement of the land of Canaan. As the Israelites' enemies were vanquished, the members of each losing nation joined the worship of the triumphant YHVH. The gods of these peoples were abandoned by their followers.

With each victory, the Israelites renewed their covenant. They would not worship the idols of other nations, and the God of Israel would protect them and bless them. And why would they worship the weak gods of their defeated foes? In addition, they owed their God a debt. YHVH had brought them out of slavery, and they owed this God their lives and their freedom. They remembered the opening words of the pact of Sinai:

> I am YHVH your God, who brought you out of the land of Egypt, out of the house of bondage: you shall have no other gods besides Me. (Exodus 20:2–3)

YHVH assimilated the attributes of each defeated deity and grew in the consciousness of the Israelites. As the fertility god Baal was destroyed, YHVH took his place and was praised as the God of the storm who sent the rain and made the crops grow. YHVH took on additional names as well. El, El Elyon, or El Shaddai, used to refer to the chief mountain god of the Canaanite pantheon, became another name for YHVH as the Israelites took control of the Canaanite high places of worship. Other names, such as Tzur, which means "Rock," and Av, which means "Father," terms used to refer to the deity of a local shrine or head of a pantheon, all became part of the worship of YHVH. As the gods of the land were defeated, YHVH took on their roles in the scope of nature. Longest to last was the concept of the goddess. Archeology has found evidence of the goddess Asherah being referred to as the wife of YHVH, just as she was once the wife of the Canaanite god El.[3]

Each name, however, also represented a different need in the people. Just as people are called different names by parents, children, and friends, so did YHVH accumulate different titles, depending upon the relationship. The kingdom of God did not just grow spatially as King David consolidated the twelve tribes of Israel into a single kingdom and expanded the borders of his rule. It also grew in the mind as the possibilities of who YHVH was, is, and could be expanded in the consciousness of the people. The progress toward monotheism, the belief in only one God in existence, was slow and frequently violent. The books of the Bible chart the course of the belief in one God for a thousand years. Fidelity to one God was only a beginning.

Hearkening back to Moses's speech, however, there was also an explicit warning in his words. After enough time in the land of Canaan, when victory was complete and the people had settled down, what would become of their loyalty then? In slavery in Egypt, the dangers of the wilderness, and the early days of settlement, the people had been solely dependent upon YHVH for their sustenance and safety. Would they become haughty with the illusory security that comes with nationhood? Would they still "hear" the demand for faithfulness to YHVH alone?

From One People to One Nation

Centuries later, many of Moses's fears had come true. The God of Israel had waged many battles, and these were recorded in the people's history. YHVH defeated Pharaoh, who was considered a god. More than that, YHVH had defeated Ra, the sun god, with a plague of darkness. The temple of Dagon of the Philistines had been pulled down by the chieftain Samson, and the zealous prophet Elijah had put the priests of the fertility god Baal to the sword.

But the Bible tells us that the people still gathered around the trees of the goddess Asherah, the wife of the king of the gods of Canaan, the High God El. They made sacrifices on mountaintops and at shrines other than Jerusalem. Worse still, some sacrificed their children to the fire-god Molech in the valley of Ben-hinnom. In the culture of the ancient Near Eastern peoples, it was normal to add new gods and goddesses to the pantheon, especially when a treaty was made. Without a clear victory or defeat, the different deities of each side would share power. It was understood that each god would not care so long as the god's needs were met through a shrine and sacrifice. It is ironic that King Solomon, King David's son who built the First Temple in Jerusalem for YHVH, also married many foreign wives to form alliances with the surrounding nations and, in doing so, invited them to bring the altars of their gods with them. For YHVH this was intolerable.[4]

Then a young king, only eight years old, named Josiah, came to the throne of Judah. In cleaning out a part of the neglected Temple of Jerusalem, the high priest, Hilkiah, came upon a scroll. He brought it to the scribe to be read. When they heard its words, they knew they had to bring this to their idealistic boy-king. Moses's words "YHVH alone" reached Josiah.

King Josiah heard these words and tore his clothes, a sign of mourning. He knew how disloyal much of his country was to their God. He consulted the prophetess Hulda, the spokesperson for YHVH, and it was confirmed. King Josiah said:

> Great indeed must be the wrath of YHVH that has been kin-
> dled against us, because our fathers did not obey the words
> of this scroll to do all that has been prescribed for us.
> (2 Kings 22:13)

In a swift and ruthless campaign, King Josiah wiped out the shrines of any deity other than YHVH. He demanded that all worship take place at one holy site, the Temple in Jerusalem, for there should be one Temple for one God in one nation. No longer would people be allowed to worship wood and stone in his kingdom. He purged his kingdom of YHVH's enemies.[5]

One God for One Nation, Even in Defeat

Much had changed in the lives of the people Israel between the time that Moses demanded their loyalty at the border of Canaan and the time of King Josiah in 622 BCE. Moses spoke to a group of people, but Josiah presided over a nation. Josiah ruled over religious, social, and political institutions susceptible to spiritual corruption. The dangers of the nation included complacency and convenience. Without the discipline of fighting for daily existence, the boundaries of the covenant became blurred by gratification and contentment.

Rarely was there a king who was completely loyal to YHVH. The boy Josiah was an exception. Many scholars believe that the scroll his high priest discovered was the book of Deuteronomy, the book of the Torah that contains the *Sh'ma*. King Josiah's reform was massive. It was an attempt to abolish the cultic practices that had infiltrated his kingdom. It was King Josiah, we are told, who even put the goddess Asherah "to the fire" (2 Kings 23:6). When King Josiah was killed in battle, however, the people reverted to idolatry. People continued to fight wars in the names of their gods. It would take greater traumas to uproot polytheism from the people's minds.[6]

Many today cannot help but be offended by the idea that belief in one God was born out of violence. Josiah's reform calls to mind modern-day barbaric purges. In biblical times, just as YHVH "passed judgment" upon other gods, so did human beings ruthlessly attack each other out of religious zeal. Such zealotry is still with us. We cannot read passages about wiping out idolaters, families and all, and not feel repulsed.

What is important to add, however, is that YHVH was also a giver of law and the spark of peoples' conscience. In addition to the fight against idolatry, the Bible details the birth of social responsibility. The commandment "You shall love your neighbor as yourself" (Leviticus 19:18) began with the God of Israel. While originally this commandment was directed solely toward a person's kinsman as an act of tribal fidelity, it was later expanded to include the stranger, as it is said in the book of Leviticus:

> When strangers reside with you in your land, you shall not wrong them. The strangers who reside with you shall be to you as your citizens; you shall love each one as yourself, for

> you were strangers in the land of Egypt. I YHVH am your
> God. (Leviticus 19:33–34)

YHVH gave many commandments regarding the treatment of others, including the humane treatment of both kin and enemies alike. With each ethical imperative came the phrase, "I am YHVH." The God of Israel was the source of moral authority and its impetus. This was slow work consisting of painful progress as the Israelites struggled to understand what their God wanted of them. The God of Israel's desire for righteousness, compassion, and peace would only become known over many centuries, and these ideals are still being negotiated into reality to this day.

Perhaps the greatest proponents of the purity of monotheism were the prophets. They were the spokespeople for YHVH who would unabashedly criticize king and Temple priest alike. They demanded not only loyalty to YHVH but also accountability to God's standard of ethics. Just as the people were not to betray YHVH with a treaty with another nation, so were they not to betray the poor and the vulnerable. The prophets Amos and Hosea would preach on behalf of God to the people in the north, and Isaiah and Jeremiah would counsel kings in the south. They would hold their monarchs responsible to the covenant of which the *Sh'ma* was a part.

As the prophets narrate the story of the Bible, they regularly depict the kings of Israel as backsliding and the people as unfaithful. More than that, the sovereignty of the kings was not to last forever. Specifically, the constant threats of Assyria and then Babylonia forced the people of Israel to rethink their faith. Eventually they would be crushed by surrounding empires with the rise and fall of military might.

It was difficult to be loyal to YHVH singularly and exclusively in victory because of the lure of self-satisfaction. We can imagine it was even more difficult in times of defeat. Yet in their defeat would come the Israelites' greatest triumph, an accomplishment of the imagination. Normally, when one people is victorious over another, the defeated group abandons their weak, defeated god and joins in worshiping the god of the victor. After all, the winner's god must be the stronger.

But this did not occur with the people of Israel. In the time of the prophets, the Israelites were eventually defeated by military means and their sovereignty destroyed, but they came up with an ingenious way of preserving their identity and their faith in YHVH. Their loss was not a matter of their God being defeated. Rather, they claimed YHVH was still superior. In fact, YHVH was simply using another nation to punish them. This defeat had nothing to do with the gods of the surrounding nations. Instead, this was an internal, family affair. YHVH was disciplining them for their sins, and when they were reconciled with their God they would become strong again. The people simply had to remember to hear the words of Moses, words that demanded loyalty to YHVH. They needed to repent:

> Let us search and examine our ways, and turn back to YHVH. Let us lift up our hearts with our hands to God in heaven. (Lamentations 3:40–41)

In defeat, the people of Israel reimagined their God as the Ruler of all nations. Their God was so powerful, God had dominion over the entire world and could even use one nation to teach another a lesson. God was the one God, the Sovereign over every kingdom. The enemies of Israel may have defeated the kingdom of Judah, but the followers of YHVH forever remade the idea of a Supreme Being.

Idolatry of the Heart

When the Israelites rejected polytheism, they also destroyed the idols in their midst. Defeating other gods meant pulling down their enemies' totems. Even as they were defeated by stronger armies and these idols were rebuilt, the prophets of Israel continued to show scorn for these objects in the name of the one God.

> Why, you are less than nothing, your effect is less than nullity; one who chooses you is an abomination. (Isaiah 41:24)

The prophet Jeremiah similarly regarded fetishism:

> They are both dull and foolish; their doctrine is but delusion; it is a piece of wood, silver beaten flat. (Jeremiah 10:8–9)

Idolatry, however, did not just include bowing down to statues. It also meant the worship of nature or of humanity itself. Moses, in the same speech as he declared the *Sh'ma,* foresaw this possibility:

> For your own sake, therefore, be most careful—since you saw no shape when YHVH your God spoke to you at Horeb out of the fire—not to act wickedly and make for yourselves a sculptured image in any likeness whatever: the form of a man or a woman, the form of any beast on earth, the form of any winged bird that flies in the sky, the form of anything that creeps on the ground, the form of any fish that is in the waters below the earth. And when you look up to the sky and behold the sun and the moon and the stars, the whole heavenly host, you must not be lured into bowing down to them or serving them. (Deuteronomy 4:15–19)

Just as people's consciousness of one God expanded to include other nations, so did their understanding of the sin of idolatry. Idolatry did not just mean the worship of forces of nature. It also came to mean the longings of the heart in ways that the one God did not desire. Worship of anything besides YHVH, material or not, was a sin and forbidden. A person could not only worship tangible objects but could also worship the personal self. Thus the prophet Jeremiah cautioned:

> Let not the wise glory in their wisdom, nor the strong glory in their strength, nor the rich glory in their riches. But only in this should one glory: in one's earnest devotion to Me. (Jeremiah 9:22–23)

The mind might idolize anything: power, fame, or prestige. The worship of wealth and status was equally idolatrous. To adore any of these things was also a betrayal of God. For Israel, YHVH was their God, YHVH alone.

The author of the book of Ecclesiastes understood idolatry in this way. All fortune eventually amounted to nothing and was not worthy of worship:

> Then my thoughts turned to all the fortune my hands had built up, to the wealth I had acquired and won—and oh, it was all futile and pursuit of wind; there was no real value under the sun! (Ecclesiastes 2:11)

The struggle against idolatry was not only manifest in the war of one people or nation against another. It was an internal struggle as well. YHVH waged a constant battle not only on behalf of the people Israel but inside of them as well. The commitment that the *Sh'ma* demanded was not just one of deed but of thought.

The God of the Universe

With the loss of the people's political power, the people became dependent upon the God of Israel again. Their understanding of God, however, had grown tremendously. As the people spread out into the Diaspora, so did their worldwide vision of God. The prophets of Israel advanced the idea that YHVH was not only a single and exclusive tribal deity of a particular territory but the one God of history over the entire world. The God of Israel was not only the God of a particular people but also the universal Sovereign of all time and space:

> My witnesses are you—declares YHVH—my servant, whom I have chosen. To the end that you may take thought, and believe in Me, and understand that I am God: Before Me no god was formed, and after Me none shall exist—none but Me, YHVH; beside Me, none can grant triumph. (Isaiah 43:10–11)

The Bible represents a thousand years of history, and a thousand years is a long time. Eventually, the last word of the *Sh'ma* would come to mean not "alone" but "one" as YHVH became not only the God of a particular people but also the only God that existed. Eventually, all would acknowledge one Power, but the prophets of Israel realized that the time when all people would realize that God is one was still far off in the future. There would come some distant day when all people would be united and all recognize that their different names referred to the same God.

If the *Sh'ma* as said by Moses is the beginning of a trajectory, its continuation is manifest in the words of the prophet Zechariah centuries later: "On that day, YHVH shall be one, and God's Name shall be one" (Zechariah 14:9). Ethical monotheism was a hard-won, gradual accomplishment, not an overnight revelation.[7]

"Hearing" Moses Today

The words of the *Sh'ma* expanded in meaning within the time of the Bible. From the demand of loyalty to a single, exclusive God to the universal Sovereign of creation and history, this statement grew in scope and depth. But do the words of the *Sh'ma* belong only to a distant place in time? Do they still ring true for us?

Certainly, humanity has grown in some ways since biblical times. While tribalism is still very much with us, we also are capable of having an understanding of the common humanity of all people. It is possible for monotheism to mean not holy war but the holiness of every person.

But idolatry is also still with us. Many of us, even the most enlightened and religious, still confuse the things that bring us power and pleasure with the things that bring us meaning and peace. Too often we confuse ego with principle, and we forget the spiritual connection that gives life purpose.

When we reject the worship of all things created and instead turn to the Creator, we continue Moses's revolution. The words of the prophet Micah are still in the process of being realized:

> God has told you, O mortal, what is good and what YHVH
> demands: to do justice, to love kindness, and to walk
> humbly with your God. (Micah 6:8)

Moses, however, was not the only one who gave his soul in this
cause. The Jewish people, with their declaration of monotheism,
would continue to struggle with the nations of the world. Many of
them, including the first sages to call themselves rabbis, would give
their lives as testimony to the one God.

שמע ישראל

Hear O Israel,

יי אלהינו

YHVH is our God,

יי אחד

YHVH is our only One!

2

The Sages Offer Their Lives

Akiba ben Joseph

A Sacred Story

A Rabbinic legend has it that God permitted Moses to look beyond his time to see who would carry the idea of one God to future generations. God transported Moses to the classroom of a Sage named Rabbi Akiba. Moses tried to follow Akiba's teaching, but he had trouble understanding the intricacies of the rabbi's lecture. Moses was reassured, however, when Akiba claimed that all of his teachings were based upon the law given to Moses at Sinai. Moses was so impressed by Akiba's erudition that he asked the Eternal why it was that Moses merited receiving the Torah when as brilliant a man as Akiba was destined to come into existence. God responded, "Be silent; such is My will." Moses also asked to see Akiba's fate and was dismayed to discover he died an old man but also a martyr. Moses again questioned God as to why such a Sage's life would end so violently. Again, God said, "Be silent; such is My will."[1] It was Akiba's destiny to die for the sake of the one God, and his death gave new meaning to the *Sh'ma*.

Rabbi Akiba ben Joseph was the most prominent sage in Judea in the second century CE, and to spot his bald head in the marketplace would have been the cause of quite a stir. The famous Rabbi was a legend in his own lifetime. People could recite his personal history by heart. In order to understand his death, it is important to understand his life.[2]

15

Akiba grew up in the aftermath of the destruction of the Second Temple of Jerusalem at the hands of the Romans. Without the Temple and its sacrificial worship, the people of Judea looked to their Sages for wisdom as to how to live.

An uneducated man, Akiba worked as a shepherd for one of the wealthiest men of the land. He fell in love with his rich employer's daughter, a young woman named Rachel. She returned his love, and they secretly married, as she knew her father would never approve. When Rachel's father found out, he cast them out of his household, and they lived in poverty.

Despite their newfound financial distress, Akiba and Rachel insisted on their children's education. Akiba would accompany his son and learn his letters alongside him. Upon seeing her husband's devotion and longing, Rachel insisted he go to the Academy of the Sages and become a disciple of the wise. Eventually, Akiba was persuaded, and off he went. He was forty years old when he started his studies.

Akiba was a dedicated student. His colleagues described Akiba's learning as similar to the way a stone cutter slowly levels a mountain, bit by bit, with great persistence. After twelve years, he was finally recognized by the Sages as one of their own. Soon his fame spread, and wealth came to him and to his wife, Rachel. Even more important than being lifted out of poverty, Akiba became a great teacher of the people. The public marveled at not only his genius and creativity but also Rachel's devotion. Their love was obvious, and some of his disciples complained that Akiba put them to shame before their wives for the affection that he showed Rachel.

Among his many teachings, Rabbi Akiba taught that each word, even each letter, of the Torah contained secrets that God intended. He preached that "Love your neighbor as yourself" was the greatest principle of the Torah. He was a master of the esoteric parts of the Jewish tradition, but the record shows that he was also willing to admit his ignorance when he did not know the answer to a question. He also made an example of his life by visiting the sick in his community. Rabbi Akiba was one of the architects of preserving Judaism after the destruction of the Temple for the next millennium.

Roman rule over the land, however, grew more harsh. The Romans did not understand Jewish practices, such as dietary laws and circumcision. In fact, they felt that the Jewish laws were backward and uncivilized. Building arenas for competitive games and carving statues of marble for the city streets, the Romans celebrated the values of power and physical beauty. In contrast, Rabbi Akiba and his colleagues preached the values of wisdom and humility. People ought to cherish inner beauty as a gift from God.

In the year 132 CE, a great soldier came to rally the people of Judea. His name was Simon bar Kozba. He felt the time was right to rebel against Rome and reclaim the land for the God of Israel. His band of followers met with dramatic success. They were victorious in Jerusalem, and Bar Kozba proclaimed himself the *Nasi*, or "Prince." So awed was Rabbi Akiba at this soldier's might, and so hopeful was he at the prospect of removing Roman oppression, that Akiba endorsed Bar Kozba as none other than the Messiah sent to free the Jewish people. Akiba renamed him "Bar Kochba," meaning "the son of a star," quoting the book of Numbers, "A star has shot out of Jacob" (Numbers 24:17). His colleagues immediately rebuked him, saying that Akiba would be long dead and buried, with grass growing over his grave, before the Messiah would truly appear.

Bar Kozba's success was short-lived. While he inflicted tremendous casualties upon the Roman legions, his army was destroyed in a matter of three years. As punishment, Jews were banned from living in Jerusalem, and the city was renamed Aelia Capitolina by the Roman emperor Hadrian, with a shrine dedicated to Jupiter in the Temple's place. The emperor also put out a ban on teaching Torah; the punishment for doing so was death.

What was Rabbi Akiba to do? He had been terribly mistaken to believe in Bar Kozba. The people were lost, and the future of the Jewish faith was imperiled. In the face of these dangers, Rabbi

Akiba continued to teach Torah. Even though some came to Akiba and begged him to stop, to save his life, Akiba refused. He had come this far in his life and worked this hard for the sake of the Torah; he simply could not give it up now under any circumstances.

Akiba was arrested, along with nine other great sages. Even in prison, people would come by Akiba's window, pretending to be selling their wares, and secretly ask him questions of Jewish law. Rabbi Akiba continued to teach under the most dire circumstances.

In the end, Rabbi Akiba was led to the gladiators' arena, the place that represented complete opposite values from the ones that Akiba preached. Before a great crowd, the Roman torturers cut into his flesh with iron combs. Around him, his students were forced to watch.

As the evening approached, Rabbi Akiba realized it was the appointed time of day to say the evening *Sh'ma*. As he stood bleeding, he explained to his students:

> All my life I have been troubled by the verse after the *Sh'ma*, which says, "You shall love YHVH your God with all your heart, with all your soul, with all your might" (Deuteronomy 6:5). With all my soul, which means even if God takes my soul. Will I be able to fulfill this commandment? Now that I can, shall I not do so?" And then Rabbi Akiba proclaimed the *Sh'ma*, elongating the last word, *echad*, "one," until he died.[3]

Prayer Replaces Sacrifice, the Home Replaces the Temple

For Akiba and the martyrs who died with him, what did the *Sh'ma* mean?

In order to understand the full force of Rabbi Akiba's pronouncement of the *Sh'ma* at his death, we must first understand how the world had changed since the time of the Bible. During the time of the Bible, people worshiped God at places of sacrifice.

People brought animals to be slaughtered, their fatty parts to be burned up in smoke amidst incense, as an offering to God. Eventually, all of the shrines in the Land of Israel were consolidated into one holy Temple in Jerusalem. This Temple was destroyed by enemies and rebuilt by the faithful, and for centuries people made pilgrimages from their homes to the Temple to offer their sacrifices and draw close to God.

The Second Temple was destroyed in the year 70 CE by the Romans, approximately when Akiba was born. Without the Temple, the Jewish people were forced to ask themselves, "How are we to worship God?" It was decided by the Sages of the time, a new brand of scholars who had mastered the Torah, that prayer could replace sacrifice. If one said prayers at the same times that sacrifices would have normally been offered up in the Temple, then this was an adequate substitute.

Further, holiday celebrations that normally would have taken place at the Temple in Jerusalem could be held in one's home. Whereas before a family would bring their paschal lamb for sacrifice to the Temple on Passover, now this holiday meal could happen in the home around the family table. The table became the family's personal altar, and the home became the center of worship.

Most importantly, the study of Torah was the centerpiece of spiritual life. To study its words was the ultimate act of worship, a dialogue with the mind of God. Central among the words of Torah was the *Sh'ma*. In fact, the great encyclopedia of Rabbinic legend and lore that the Sages left for future generations, the Babylonian Talmud, begins with the words; "From when may we recite the *Sh'ma* in the evening?"[4]

The Rabbis formulated many laws about how people needed to say the *Sh'ma*. It was not allowed to say this prayer in an unclean place. The words had to be said with proper concentration and distinctive pronunciation of the letters. If a person did not say the words audibly, however, God's commandment of saying the *Sh'ma* was still fulfilled so long as the person's intention was sincere. A person was also allowed to say the *Sh'ma* in any language that he or she understood. The most important principle was that the worshiper had to be disciplined as to the times when the *Sh'ma* should be said, for the Torah commanded that these words should be said "when you lie down and when you rise up" (Deuteronomy 6:7). By following such a routine, the worshiper was imitating the practices that once took place in the Temple.[5]

Would this new form of worship be as effective as the cultic practices of the past? Many were not sure. The Temple was understood to be the center of the universe, the place where heaven touched earth and where God forgave the people for their sins on Yom Kippur. Some even believed that it was the foundation of the world, that without it the world would literally come to an end. Could prayer and spiritual deeds keep them connected to God and keep the world going? The Rabbis insisted that the answer was yes, so long as the people were committed and diligent. The people had to study the Torah, day and night, as the sacred word of God. They had to recite the *Sh'ma* every morning and every evening, and they had to conduct themselves with their deeds as if they were priests of the Temple. In doing so, they made their Temple portable, in that they carried the spirit of the Temple with them in the scrolls of the Torah. God, in a sense, became portable as well, hearkening back to the times of the Tabernacle in the wilderness.

> It occurred as Rabbi Jochanan ben Zakkai was leaving Jerusalem [when the Temple was destroyed], Rabbi Joshua followed after him and saw the Temple in ruins. "What a horror for us," Rabbi Joshua said, "that this, the place where the sins of Israel were atoned for, is utterly ruined!"
>
> "My son," Rabbi Jochanan said, "do not mourn. We have another means of atonement as effective as this. What is it? It is acts of loving kindness, as it is said, 'For I desire mercy and not sacrifice.'" (Hosea 6:6)[6]

The Rabbis believed in one God, and they believed that spiritual actions, such as prayer and repentance, would connect them to their God.[7] To say the *Sh'ma*, therefore, was a way to bring the worship of God's Temple into their hearts; doing so regularly helped maintain the foundation of the world. Ultimately, it is the *Sh'ma*, the belief in a Supreme Being who is available in every time and place through devotion to the covenant made at Sinai, that links biblical and Rabbinic Judaism.

Only One God, Even If It Means Risking Your Life

According to Jewish law as formulated by the Rabbis, there are only three good reasons for sacrificing your own life.[8] The first is to choose to die rather than commit murder. Given the choice between sacrificing our own life versus taking another's, we are forbidden to purposefully murder another human being. "Who knows whose blood is redder?" ask the Sages.[9]

The second reason is to avoid committing a sexual crime. Rather than commit rape or some other kind of sexual violation, we are to offer our lives first.

The third sin that Jews are commanded to martyr themselves rather than commit is to perform public idolatry. For the Sages, to deny God in public was to rob life of its meaning.

We may understand the first two reasons, for murder and rape are so obviously heinous to us that many of us would instinctively refuse to do so, even if it meant endangering ourselves. The third, however, may seem foreign. Why such a fuss over denying God? Can't we simply repent later, seeing as how we were acting under duress?

The answer is yes and no. Yes, people who denied God were always given a chance to repent. Sometimes people are forced to say what they do not mean, even if it strikes to the core of what they believe. This is why if an individual is forced to worship an idol in private in order to save his or her life, the Sages say this is permissible. The act takes place only between that person and God.

But the Rabbis were concerned that if the Jews were to publicly deny God, this might lead to widespread surrender of their values and traditions. This could mean, during a time of peril, the end of Judaism. And Jewish civilization, the Rabbis believed, was worth dying for.

When the Romans forbade the study of Torah and forced their pagan customs onto the Jewish people, Akiba continued to teach. For him to stop would have been seen as an act of public idolatry, as a denial of God. Legend has it that people pleaded with him to stop and save his life, saying that they already knew what was truly in his heart. Yet for Rabbi Akiba, a man who had already given up his former life as a shepherd to become a sage, a man who spent years away from his beloved wife to study and become the man she dreamed of, a man who had given his soul to a spiritual quest and had even endorsed a rebellion, denying the God of Israel was simply impossible. Rabbi Akiba explained his situation to the people:

> I can explain my actions by means of a parable: A fox was trotting by a river bank and, seeing fish swimming about frantically, asked them, "From whom are you escaping?" They replied, "From the nets and hooks fishermen have set for us." So the fox said to them, "Would you like to come up onto the dry land, and we will live together?" They answered, "You, fox, may be considered the cleverest of animals, but you cannot fool us. If we are afraid in the place where we can stay alive, how much more afraid should we be in a place where we will certainly die!" Thus it is with us. If we are afraid when we sit and study the Torah, of which it is written, "It is your life and the length of your days" (Deuteronomy 30:20), how much more afraid should we be if we stop studying the Torah![10]

For Rabbi Akiba and the Sages, life without the Torah was simply not worth living. While we might question for ourselves whether or not we might have done the same, we can only wonder at their faith.

Saying the *Sh'ma* as Protest

Akiba, however, was doing more than affirming his own faith when he said the *Sh'ma* as he died. He also was protesting against the immorality around him.

While the Romans brought their Hellenistic heritage of order, technology, and art to the lands that they had conquered, they also brought values that were in direct conflict with Judaism. Just as Judaism was moving away from cultic sacrifice and moving toward prayer and study, the Romans wanted to institute their own form of pagan worship. The fact that the gods of Rome were pleased when gladiators fought tigers and each other in bloody spectacles, that idolatrous shrines were erected on the city streets, that people bowed down to the image of the Caesar, and that prostitutes sold themselves to nobles in public only served to alienate the Jewish people. Add to this the Roman beliefs that circumcision was a desecration of the human body and keeping *kashrut* (ritualized eating according to priestly laws) was a form of primitivism, and the result was inevitably explosive.

Akiba made the daring move of endorsing Bar Kozba as the Messiah to throw off Roman rule. Bar Kozba would most likely not have received the tremendous following that he did had not a sage as great as Akiba lent him his support. Rabbi Akiba, however, was immediately rebuked by his colleagues for doing so, and he soon saw his tremendous folly. Rome was not to be defeated by military means.

In choosing martyrdom, Rabbi Akiba acted out of spiritual resistance. Rome's physical power could not be overcome, but that did not mean the Jewish people had to surrender their souls. When Akiba said the *Sh'ma* and said that he now had the opportunity to fulfill the commandment to love God with all of his soul, he was doing more than giving himself over to God. He was also denying the Romans power over his soul, affirming that the one God, and only the one God, was worth dying for. Death was not for the entertainment of a cheering crowd in a coliseum.

Akiba taught that "human beings are loved because they were made in God's image."[11] This image was the morality that they displayed in their behavior, not physical beauty or power. Akiba attempted to demonstrate Jewish values as taught by his circle in the face of Roman culture. His *Sh'ma* was a protest on behalf of God. With his death, he affirmed what his predecessor, a sage named Hillel, preached:

> In a place where no one behaves like a human being, you must strive to be human![12]

One God in the World-to-Come

The legend of Rabbi Akiba's death has an additional ending. It is said that upon his death, ending his life with the word *echad,* that God is one, a heavenly voice broke forth. It is recorded in the Talmud that the divine voice said, "Happy are you, Akiba, that your soul departed with the word *echad!*"[13]

The angels, however, were shocked. They turned toward God and asked, "Such is the Torah, and such is its reward?" A righteous man such as Akiba did not deserve such a fate. He deserved to have died quietly in his bed, taken by God and not at the hand of an enemy. God explained to them that this was Rabbi Akiba's portion in this world, but he had a greater portion in the world-to-come.

The Rabbis believed in a version of heaven. They believed that there was a place for the righteous, especially for the Sages, to sit at a table amidst shining light and study Torah with none other than Moses himself. This was what they meant by the world-to-come.

In addition to this, there was another kind of a world of the future, a world on this earth that had to be built through effort and sometimes through sacrifice. This world is the world as it should be under God's rule. The phrase "world-to-come" sometimes means a heavenly abode, but it also could mean the earthly world of the future, a world founded on justice, compassion, and peace.

Rabbi Akiba martyred himself to affirm that one day morality would triumph. God's sovereignty and unity would one day be acknowledged by all. The fact that we are still studying his teachings and learning from his words today is part of Rabbi Akiba's portion. Our present time is a step toward Rabbi Akiba's world-to-come. We know, however, that the realization of this future world is slow in arriving. Centuries of Jewish history contain great sacrifice.

Generations of Jews who were martyrs also knew Rabbi Akiba's story and drew strength from it. Most prominent among these were the Jews of Europe who died at the hands of the Crusaders. The First Crusade (1095–1099) was especially bloody, and many Jews, when all hope was lost before the oncoming mob, chose to kill their families and then themselves rather than be tortured to death. In doing so, we have testimonies that many declared the *Sh'ma*, imitating Rabbi Akiba.[14]

These prayers were not utterances of complete despair. One rabbi in France who lived through the First Crusade, a famous commentator and teacher named Rabbi Solomon ben Isaac (called by the acronym of this name, Rashi, 1040–1105), knew well his community's dying declaration. Nevertheless, he had this to say about the *Sh'ma*:

> "YHVH is our God" now and not [acknowledged as] the God of the other nations, [but] in the future will be "YHVH the One" [of all the peoples], as it is said, "For then I will make the peoples pure of speech, so that they all invoke YHVH by name and serve God as one" (Zephaniah 3:9),

and "On that day, YHVH shall be one, and God's Name shall be one" (Zechariah 14:9).[15]

According to these martyrs, the *Sh'ma*, ending with the word *echad*, "one," will one day reach its fulfillment. One day, not only will God be acknowledged as one, but all the people of the earth will be one as well.

"Hearing" Akiba: We Remember You, O Father Israel

In the synagogue, when the congregation sings the *Sh'ma*, a phrase traditionally follows it in a whisper, "Blessed be the Name whose glorious majesty is forever and ever."

The Rabbis taught that when the patriarch Jacob lay dying, a special moment occurred between him and his sons. Jacob, whose other name was Israel, a name given to him by an angel, called out and gathered his twelve sons around him. These twelve sons would one day be the heads of the twelve tribes of Israel. And yet, Jacob was filled with anxiety.

"What if one of my sons fails to remember what we have gone through on behalf of God?" Jacob wondered. "What if one of them will not keep the faith?" His sons assured him of their faithfulness. They said, "Listen, O father Israel, YHVH is our God, YHVH our only one! Just as in your heart there is only one, so in our hearts there is only one." Their father Israel then blessed them in his dying voice, no more than a whisper: "Blessed be the Name whose glorious majesty is forever and ever."[16]

In this parable, the Rabbis understand the word "Israel" in the *Sh'ma* to literally refer to the man named Israel, the patriarch Jacob. But in spirit it also refers to all those who came before us who kept faith with God and sometimes even gave their lives for the One. They did so that others might live in the true worship of YHVH and practice the moral deeds that God demands.

Part of what it means to hear the *Sh'ma* is to recognize the martyrs of the Jewish people and not to let them have died in vain. We hear the voice of Akiba and others like him who went through hell for our sake, and by reciting the *Sh'ma* with true devotion, we remember them and we remember our God.

שמע ישראל

Hear O Israel,

יי אלהינו

YHVH is our God,

יי אחד

YHVH the one Creator!

3

Proving the One

Saadia Gaon

A Sacred Story

He had been deposed.

The great Jewish scholar of Babylonia of the ninth and tenth centuries, Saadia Gaon, had just received word. He had been declared by the leader of the community, the exilarch David ben Zakkai, to no longer be the Gaon, or the head of the Academy of Sura. His enemies in the Jewish establishment had appealed to none other than the Muslim authorities, going as high as the caliph himself, to get him removed from office. These ungrateful people were the very ones he had helped reach prominence. He felt betrayed.

Saadia recovered quickly. He still had his allies. The scholars in his academy were still loyal to him, and he had wealthy bankers at his side. He did not sit still long; it was not his way. He devised a strategy and then did what no one had done before.

Instead of simply leaving quietly, Saadia Gaon retaliated. He refused to give up his title, Gaon, which literally meant "genius." He made a proclamation: "It is not that I am removed as the Gaon of the Academy. It is I who will remove the exilarch from power."

Saadia staged a revolt. The exilarch was the secular leader of the Jewish community in Babylonia, a man who had great power. To replace him, Saadia audaciously appointed his own brother, a man named Josiah, to be the new exilarch. It was sheer daring that

Saadia would have the courage to declare a replacement for someone who ranked higher than he.

The controversy would last for several years. Unfortunately,
this was not a good time for the Jewish community to show weak-
ness. Muslims, Christians, and others regularly challenged the
beliefs of the Jewish people. Now, with the split between Saadia
Gaon and the exilarch, the community of Israel in Babylonia was a
house divided.

Saadia Gaon could not govern his academy amidst the years
of chaos. Disunity raged against him from without and from
within. The revolt was essentially a failure.

And so Saadia did the only thing he could do. He sat down,
and he wrote. He would prove his ideological opponents wrong,
whether they be of another religion or dissenters within the Jewish
community, by his scholarship. He would prove once and for all
that he could demonstrate the one true way toward the one God.
He would show them the way through the light of reason.

While in political isolation, Saadia Gaon took his quill and
penned these words about those he saw around him:

> When, now, I considered these fundamentals and the evil
> resulting therefrom, my heart was grieved for my species,
> the species of rational beings, and my soul was stirred on
> account of our people, the children of Israel. For I saw in
> this age of mine many believers whose belief was not pure
> and whose convictions were not sound, whilst many of the
> deniers of faith boasted of their corruption and looked
> down upon the devotees of the truth although they were
> themselves in error. I saw, furthermore, men who were
> sunk, as it were, in seas of doubt and overwhelmed by waves
> of confusion and there was no diver to bring them up from
> the depths nor a swimmer who might take hold of their
> hands and carry them ashore....
>
>   As for the fact that God is one, this is expressed in the
> statement in Scripture, "Hear O Israel, YHVH is our God,

YHVH is one!" (Deuteronomy 6:4), as well as in its statement, "See now I, even I, am God, and there is no god with Me" (Deuteronomy 32:9), and its statement, "YHVH alone did lead him, and there was no strange god alongside," (Deuteronomy 32:12).[1]

In order to understand Saadia Gaon's quotation of the *Sh'ma*, it is necessary to understand the polemical nature of his writing and the reasons behind it. Saadia Gaon eventually reclaimed his authority through rational discourse and through repeated citations of Scripture, the very Scripture that those of other religions sought to use for their own ends. He would seek to overpower them with his clarity and diligence, and so pull out those who were drowning "in seas of doubt." By doing so, he would also force his authority as a scholar onto his political opponents and retrieve his appointment.[2]

The *Sh'ma* as Polemic: Challenges from All Sides

Saadia ben Joseph, better known as Saadia Gaon (882–942), was a fighter born into a time of great religious conflicts. A broader perspective on his life will give more meaning to what he meant when he said the *Sh'ma*.

Centuries before, Christians had announced in Constantinople the belief in the Trinity, that God was one but simultaneously three Persons: the Father, the Son, and the Holy Spirit. This doctrine became accepted as standard in both Western as well as Eastern Orthodox Christianity.

In addition, the caliphs of the family of Mohammed the Prophet spread the faith of Islam throughout the Middle East. The Abbasid Empire began in the year 750 CE and would last for almost two centuries. The Abbasids made the capital of their power in Baghdad, coincidentally very close to the two main academies of Jewish learning in Sura and Pumbeditha. Most importantly, the works of Aristotle and other Greek philosophers were translated into Arabic and were now widespread, and Islamic philosophers debated their contents. Philosophical doctrines, once "brushed away as with a reed,"[3] were now part of the intellectual elite.

And within Judaism itself, a sect of people had broken off, calling themselves Karaites, who denied the authority of the Rabbis and claimed a more literal reading of the Torah as the only legitimate path of Judaism. While little is known about the founder of the sect, a man named Anan ben David, later Karaite thinkers proved to be influential opponents of Rabbinic Judaism. Among the Jewish people themselves there were doubters about Rabbinic authority. When Saadia recited the Sh'ma, therefore, he was declaring it in the face of these ideological opponents. He faced challenges to his belief all his life.

When Saadia was born in 882 CE in Egypt, he was raised and grew with what must have been a remarkable education. He was exposed to Trinitarianism in Christianity and the beliefs of the dominant Islamic culture that surrounded him, and he had already written a polemic against the Karaites before the age of twenty-three. He traveled through the Land of Israel and up to Aleppo, and eventually he came to the famous Babylonian academies, where he was recognized as a man of great learning. Saadia took it upon himself to write a defense of traditional Judaism, refuting the challenges that came to him from all sides. He was more than willing to give those he considered inferior a good tongue-lashing.

The exilarch David ben Zakkai had been warned that Saadia was "fearless," but appointed him as Gaon anyway. Saadia was also controversial because he was a foreigner, having come from Egypt. The exilarch lived to regret his decision, and it took a great deal of effort to get Saadia out of his position. During this exile from office, however, Saadia wrote his most insightful works and sharp polemics.

The most important work that Saadia produced during his time of political exile was called *The Book of Beliefs and Opinions*. It is the first book in Jewish history that tries to bolster Judaism's claims of faith with reason. In the book, Saadia does not just want to prove that Judaism's claim that God is one is true. He also wants to prove that all of his philosophical opponents are wrong. Saadia takes careful aim at Christians, who claimed that God is three persons in one; at Aristotelians, who claimed that the world was eternal; and at the Karaites, who interpreted the Bible in a more literal fashion than the Rabbis. By defeating these "deniers of faith," Saadia would emerge victorious and once again at the head of the Babylonian Jewish community.

Saadia finished the book and was reinstated as Gaon five years later, but this was mainly through reconciliation with his enemies. He would live for only five more years after that, dying in the year 942 CE.

Saadia's Four Proofs of a Creator

When Saadia recited the *Sh'ma,* he was not only making a declaration of faith. He also felt that he was pronouncing what he felt was the logical truth if people would have the discipline to reason the matter out. His statement of the *Sh'ma* was a philosophical declaration, and it was a polemic against the forces that were arrayed against him. Saadia believed that reason not only did not contradict faith but strengthened it.

Saadia sought to prove that the world could only have come into being by a single Creator, and if that was the case, then there could be only one God. Whereas there were many around him who believed that the world was eternal, or at least that heaven was, or that the world was created through a number of divine beings, Saadia sought to prove once and for all that there was one God who created everything out of nothing. When Saadia said the *Sh'ma,* he was really saying, "Hear O Israel, YHVH is our God, YHVH is the one indivisible Creator!" He felt that if he could prove this point and tie it to Scripture, he would have affirmed the truth of Judaism.

How do we know something, such as the unity of God, is true? Saadia claimed that there were four sources of knowledge in the world: sense perception, intuition, logic, and a reliable tradition.[4] Using these tools, he set out to prove that there could be only one Creator of the universe, not only because tradition dictated it through the *Sh'ma,* but because the senses, intuition, and logic demanded it. The doctrines of his opponents, Saadia claimed, were simply false.

The Book of Beliefs and Opinions presents four demonstrations or "proofs" that there is one Creator of the whole universe. Each one of these proofs takes on a different perspective on the world.[5]

In the first proof, Saadia claims that if we were to look up from the earth to the heavens, we might think that they go on forever. The earth and the heavens, however, are finite things. They rotate and are limited, with a beginning and an end. This being the case, something greater than they must have put the heavens and the earth in motion, for a finite thing cannot move itself forever. Some one force of infinite power must keep all the parts of the universe moving around, because they cannot move themselves, for all finite things eventually come to a stop.

For the second proof of God as Creator, Saadia asks us not to look up at the heavens but to look within. Every being, every thing, is made of parts. Sometimes these parts are connected, and sometimes they are separate. These composite things are linked and combined in extraordinary ways with a design too great to simply happen spontaneously. Something separate from them must join them and disconnect them, something that is external to all matter.

For the third proof, Saadia asks us to look at another dimension. Rather than look up or within, Saadia asks us to observe the world around us. Every living thing has characteristics, and these characteristics change. Animals and plants grow and change; things change color, temperature, and height; and people grow old and die. As all things come and go, there must be one stable thing outside of it all that causes these changes. The world must be founded on something that is immune to change so that all else can exist.

Finally, for the fourth proof, Saadia asks us to look at the dimension of time. Time, Saadia claims, can be broken up into moments. The most obvious of these is past, present, and future. If time were infinite, then breaking things up into moments would be impossible if not meaningless. There would be no past, present, or future, and there would not even be a right now, this very instant, in which we exist. We would not be able to think back in time with memory, nor could time reach us in the here and now. As we do exist right now, however, and we do know that we live in a moment, then time itself must be finite, with a beginning and an end. Something outside of time must have started it.

Saadia insists that whether we look up at the heavens, or deep within among all our intricate parts, or at the path of life with all of its characteristics and changes, or at time itself, some one power outside of it all must have set these things in motion. All things eventually wear out and disintegrate. If all things eventually disappear, then they must have originally appeared some time in the past, for these limited things could not have made themselves. One Being, known to us as God, must have made them.

For Saadia, using the science of his day, the *Sh'ma* was the logical conclusion of any rational being. The existence of one God was not to be believed just because Scripture said so or because people witnessed miracles from long ago. We can believe in one God because the idea of a Creator makes sense. Beyond space above or within, beyond changes over time or time itself, all things come and go. Creation, with all its limitations and myriad parts, implies the existence of something beyond time and space and change: a One.

Saadia must have had in mind his predecessor, Rabbi Akiba, who also posited the existence of one Creator, as recorded in the Rabbinic legend. This parable regarding an incident involving Akiba reads:

> It happened that a heretic came to Rabbi Akiba and asked,
> "Who created the world?" Rabbi Akiba replied, "The Holy

Blessed One." The heretic said, "Prove it to me." Rabbi Akiba replied, "Come back to me tomorrow."

The next day, when the heretic came, Rabbi Akiba asked him, "What are you wearing?" The heretic replied, "A garment." Rabbi Akiba asked, "Who made it?" The heretic said, "A weaver." "I do not believe you," said Rabbi Akiba. "Prove it to me." The heretic said, "What kind of proof can I show you? Do you not know that of course a weaver made it?" Rabbi Akiba then asked; "And you, do you not know that the Holy One made this world?"

After the heretic left, Rabbi Akiba's disciples asked him, "But what is the real proof?" Akiba taught, "My students, even as a house implies a builder, a garment a weaver, or a door a carpenter, so does the world imply that the Holy One of Blessing made it."[6]

Saadia felt he was upholding the long-established truth of Judaism by proving the existence of one indivisible Creator. He was continuing the tradition of Moses, Akiba, and others before him, but he was putting this truth into the language of his day. Saadia felt the need to translate the implications of the *Sh'ma* for the challenges of his generation.

One Author

Saadia's efforts may not have ultimately helped him politically, but they did have long-reaching implications beyond his lifetime. Generations of Jews would look back at his endeavor to prove the existence of one God as the Creator of the world and be inspired in their own belief. Among these, the philosopher Bachya ibn Pakuda, who lived a century and a half later and as far away as Spain, continued Saadia's tradition of proving the One.

For Bachya, like his predecessor, the *Sh'ma* was a statement of faith. Bachya makes this clear when he says, "First there is the command to believe in the Creator, when it says, 'Hear O Israel,

YHVH.... ' In using the word *Sh'ma,* the text refers not to hearing with the ear, but to inward belief."[7] Bachya felt the *Sh'ma* meant to wholeheartedly accept the unity of God the Creator.

Continuing Saadia's work, Bachya summarizes his belief with a beautiful analogy. He asks us to imagine that someone comes to us with a piece of paper with some lines of writing on it. That person then tells us that he or she spilled ink onto the paper, and the writing spontaneously happened by itself!

> Do you not realize that if ink were poured out accidentally on a blank sheet of paper, it would be impossible that proper writing should result, legible lines such as are written by a pen? If a person brought us a fair copy of script that could only have been written with a pen, and said that ink had been spilt on paper and these written characters had come of themselves, we would charge him to his face with falsehood, for we would feel certain that this result could not have happened without any intelligent person's purpose. Since this appears to us an impossibility in the case of characters the form of which is conventional, how can one assert that something far finer in its art and which manifests in its fashioning a subtlety infinite beyond our comprehension could have happened without purpose, power, and wisdom of a wise and mighty designer?[8]

If we would refuse to believe that words could write themselves with ink on paper and must have been written by someone, then certainly something much more complicated like the physics of the universe also must have an Author. Moreover, the fact that words, and the world, can have meaning and wisdom implies that there is purpose to our existence here on earth, created by the one God.

The image of God as an Author speaks especially to Judaism, for Jews have long been obsessed with words. According to Genesis, God created the world by speaking words, such as "Let there be light!" (Genesis 1:3). Similarly, the book in Bachya's analogy is existence itself, and we are compelled to perceive its Author in humility and gratitude.

"Hearing": Do We Believe in a Creator?

Today, some of us might flinch at the polemics of religious thinkers. As with Saadia, religion often becomes intertwined with politics, and people use terms like "Intelligent Design" for their own agendas. We are rightly suspicious of those who claim to be the sole keepers of truth, who have moved beyond any doubt into the realm of religious certainty. Such certainty, we feel, lacks humility that our minds are only able to grasp something of this universe, and we are very small in the scheme of things. Our faith ought to make us skeptical of our own knowledge.

Nevertheless, we can appreciate that Saadia and those like him insisted that we not simply accept claims on faith but that we use the minds that God gave us to think things through. Rather than simply throw up our hands and surrender to the mysteries of the world, we can make progress and grow in understanding. Saadia refused to accept the faith claims of others and wanted his belief to be founded not only by faith and tradition but also by reason. True, if faith ever contradicted reason, he would automatically side with what he believed from tradition. But Saadia demanded that we try to bolster our beliefs with rational thought as best we can.

To "hear" Saadia and those like him is to believe that God wants us to pursue the idea of God's unity with our intellects. Rather than blindly accept what has been handed to us on faith alone, we ought to try to reason out the claims of religion for ourselves. Religion and science, Saadia claimed, need not be mutually exclusive. We can hear God with both our hearts and our heads.

Saadia's understanding of the *Sh'ma* challenges us with questions: Do we believe in a Creator? When we look at the grandeur of nature, containing mountains, canyons, and stars, as well as experiences like childbirth, does something stir inside of us? What of "simpler," everyday things, such as the human body or the wing of a bird? How do more recent discoveries, such as the parts of the atom or the Big Bang Theory, impact our belief? In short, what do we make of these laws of nature that can bring us everything from extraordinary vistas to deadly hurricanes?

Can we "hear" God through the world around us?

שמע ישראל

Hear O Israel,

יי אלהינו

YHVH is our God,

יי אחד

YHVH is wholly unique!

4

Nothing Like God

Moses Maimonides

A Sacred Story

Rabbi Moses ben Maimon (1135–1204) sat at his desk. His home was in Fostat, outside of Cairo. It was a relief to finally be at home. His work as a physician was tiring. His mornings were spent with the sultan, treating members of the royal court for any physical complaints that they might have. Most of them were matters of simply not eating well, and time and again he begged them to eat a healthy diet.

In the afternoons he would return home and see the people of his community, treating their ailments as well. And when evening finally came, he would teach, often being consulted on religious and philosophical matters. By this time he could hardly stand, and he would lie on his side and try to get something to eat and drink.

During the night, pushing off the few hours of sleep that he would allow himself, the rabbi would write. Treatises on Jewish law, essays on the correct beliefs of Jewish faith, and letters answering questions from around the world flowed from his prolific pen.[1]

The letter before him at this moment, however, was special. It was to a student who used to live near him in Egypt, a young rabbi named Joseph ben Rabbi Judah. The young man was perplexed. This pupil was not confused because he was stubborn or lazy. Quite the opposite. Rabbi Joseph was a diligent scholar. He had mastered the arts of poetry, astronomy, mathematics, and logic, all of the basics of a fine education. He was also pious, having a firm command of the Bible, Talmud, and Jewish law. Rabbi Joseph was perplexed, however, because he had reached as far as his standard schooling could take him. He had read the works of so-called rational Jewish scholars, but their conclusions did not come together. There were too many places where science and religion contradicted each other. Rabbi Joseph wrote to his teacher in desperation. What was he to do?

It had been years since Rabbi Joseph had moved away. Nevertheless, the young man had continued his studies. His teacher was thrilled that he had not given up but had continued to pursue matters of higher learning. More than that, Rabbi Moses ben Maimon missed him. It seemed like yesterday that Rabbi Moses's brother David had been taken from him in a terrible drowning accident, and he longed for brotherly companionship. His student had given his teacher more than he would ever understand.

Delighting in receiving his inquisitive pupil's letters, Rabbi Moses took the time to respond. Finding energy for such a wonderful young mind, the world-renowned philosopher had spent months and months writing a guide for his student, sending it to him chapter by chapter. Rabbi Moses ben Maimon's treatise was, in many ways, the culmination of a life's worth of thinking. Like Saadia Gaon before him, he, too, sought to prove the unity of God, but he also went beyond him in method as well as the scope of other subjects.

Central to his treatise was the implication of the truth of one God as stated in the *Sh'ma*.[2] As he finished his latest chapter, he put the pages of parchment into one pile. He rolled it and sealed it with wax, the recognizable seal of a famous scholar. His words are difficult to grasp:

> When we wish to indicate that the deity is [one and] not many, the one who makes the statement cannot say anything but that He is one, even though "one" and "many" are

some of the subdivisions of quantity. For this reason, we give the gist of the notion and give the mind the correct direction toward the true reality of the matter when we say, one but not through oneness, just as we say eternal in order to indicate that He has not come into being in time.... When we say *one*, the meaning is that He has no equal and not that the notion of oneness attaches to His essence.[3]

With these words, Rabbi Moses ben Maimon would claim that God is so utterly transcendent that even the words "one" and "eternal" are ultimately inadequate. His claim would be that human language simply cannot say anything definitive about God but only "give the mind correct direction."

The man who thinkers during the Renaissance would call Moses Maimonides composed his greatest work, *The Guide for the Perplexed,* for his student, Rabbi Joseph, and for others like him, "however few they are."[4] It caused an uproar in the world of Judaism for centuries, and some rabbis even banned his books. The idea of God being "one" would never be the same after a person had read Maimonides. If he had lived to see the result of his work, Maimonides would probably have been pleased with the outcome. If only a few students would understand the secrets and true implications of God's oneness, then he would have been satisfied.

A God with No Image or Body

For Maimonides, educated Jews of his era could not help but be perplexed when they recited the *Sh'ma.* They ought to have been perplexed because there was a paradox inherent in Judaism and in the Torah that had not yet been faced, and many people did not have the courage to confront the issue.

The problem was that the Torah, on the one hand, talks about God being one and having no image or body. God is simply one, and it is forbidden to make an idol, as it says in the second of the Ten Commandments: "You shall not make for yourself a sculptured image or any likeness of what is in the heavens above, or on the earth below, or in the waters under the earth" (Exodus 20:4).

On the other hand, the very same Torah talks about God in many places as if God has a body. When God divides the Sea of Reeds, the Torah says, "At the blast of Your nostrils the waters piled up" (Exodus 15:8) as if God has a nose. God walks with Noah (Genesis 6:9) as if God has legs, and even goes out strolling in the Garden of Eden "at the breezy time of day" (Genesis 3:8) as if God prefers a cool wind during exercise. God sits on a throne in front of the prophet Isaiah, wearing a robe (Isaiah 6:1). The Torah says God has feet (Exodus 24:10), fingers (Exodus 31:18), hands (Exodus 9:3), eyes (Genesis 38:7), and ears (Numbers 11:1). Maimonides points out that there are many examples where the Torah contradicts itself, demanding first that we have no image of God and yet then describing God in anthropomorphic terms, as if God has a body.

Maimonides holds that the writing of the Torah is true, but it cannot contradict anything that reason demonstrates is impossible. If there is a contradiction in the Torah with what we understand, then the problem is that we are not understanding the Torah properly. Unlike Saadia and previous thinkers who know what they believe on faith and use reason to justify their belief, Maimonides is willing to risk trying to discover what is true. Whatever is the truth, whether discovered through Scripture or through logic, that is what the Torah must have intended. God speaks to us in the Torah in human terms that we can understand, but the truth is much more profound. We have to rethink what the Torah is saying, even if we understand its words in a radically different way than the norm. Maimonides therefore asks that we understand these images as metaphors or teaching devices to help the human mind get a better sense of what it is that God truly does. The one God may not really have a body, but nevertheless, we can come closer to what God is by using images that the mind can grasp.

For instance, Maimonides spends a great deal of time in the *Guide* redefining biblical terms. When human beings "go down," it means that they descend, fall, or walk downward. When God "goes down" to Mount Sinai, however, the words "go down" have to mean something categorically different, because God does not have a body with legs or even wings, for that matter, to physically come down. Instead, Maimonides teaches that God "going down" to Mount Sinai is a metaphor, a way of saying that the event of prophecy began for Moses on top of the mountain. Nothing physically happened, but rather, a mental event occurred inside of Moses on the mountain that the Torah describes to us as "going down." We have this imagery so our minds can try to understand the implications of the event.[5]

Similarly, when the Bible says God sits on a throne, it does not mean that God physically sits in a castle on a fancy chair. The throne is a symbol of dignity, honor, and moral supremacy. The image of the throne stirs up emotions within us so that we get a sense of the values the Torah is teaching, but not anything about what God actually is like.[6]

The problem, however, is deeper than this. If God really is one, indivisible, without an image or body, then what can we say that God truly does? What characteristics can we possibly assign to God? Does this mean that God did not really physically appear to the prophets or speak to our ancestors? How are we supposed to pray to something we cannot imagine? Maimonides is insistent that these depictions in the Torah are figurative descriptions, not to be taken literally. To be "one" is to be beyond physical characteristics or body parts. There is no "essential attribute" that we can attach to God such as being tall, short, mighty, kind, or any other kind of characteristic. Nor are there any parts into which we can divide God, such as hands, feet, or even dimensions such as up and down. All such words are ultimately human. God is utterly and simply one, and God's oneness defies human language. He explains:

> If, however, you belong to those whose aspirations are directed toward ascending to that high rank which is the rank of speculation, and to gaining certain knowledge with regard to God's being One by virtue of true Oneness, so

that no composition whatever is to be found in Him and no possibility of division in any way whatever—then you must know that He, may He be exalted, has in no way and in no mode any essential attribute, and that just as it is impossible that He should be a body, it is also impossible that He should possess an essential attribute.[7]

In sum, there are no words for God that work. God is beyond description. There is nothing that we can truly say about God.

This kind of rereading of the Bible is demanding and not for everyone. Some might feel that it leaves them cold, that they need their God to be more emotionally evocative, even comforting. We want God to appear as a pillar of fire at the defense of the Israelites, to physically talk to Abraham, and to appear to Moses from the midst of a burning bush. We like the pictures that the miracles of the Bible give us, and demystifying them might feel like a loss. Maimonides, however, is relentless in his intellectual integrity. If God is one and has no body or form, then this must apply everywhere, all the time. If we can get past this emotional loss, Maimonides says, then saying the *Sh'ma* will be more honest.

You shall be one of those who represent to themselves the unity of the Name and not one of those who merely proclaim it with their mouth without representing to themselves that it has a meaning.[8]

Nothing Like God: Wholly Unique

Maimonides was intellectually uncompromising about the oneness of God. To believe in one God is a commandment of Judaism. "This God is One," Maimonides wrote in his code of Jewish law. "God's oneness is such that there is not a oneness like it in the world."[9]

What Maimonides seems to have meant when he said the *Sh'ma* is that God is one and there is nothing like God in all the universe. Nothing can be compared to God. It is not that God is "the most high" or "the tallest" or "the most powerful." These are comparisons of degree. Maimonides seems to be saying that God is categorically something else, that it is not a matter of difference by degree but of kind. These words are human words and therefore limited. God, however, is not bound by human limitations. We do not even have a basis of comparison with which to liken God. "To whom, then, can you liken Me, to whom can I be compared?—says the Holy One.... My thoughts are not your thoughts, and my ways are not your ways" (Isaiah 40:25, 55:8).

In other words, Maimonides taught that when we say the *Sh'ma* and say that God is one, what we might really be saying is that God is unique, unlike anything else on earth. This might be the true definition of the Hebrew word *echad*.

We can object and say: So what? Everything is unique. I am unique, and you are unique. To be unique means to have at least one characteristic that nothing else shares. Every table and chair is essentially unique. So what if God is unique?

Maimonides, however, is saying something more. God, Maimonides proclaims with the *Sh'ma,* is wholly unique. God does not share even a single characteristic with anything else. God simply is. We do not have adequate language to truthfully add a predicate to this sentence if we insist on being rationally consistent. Not even the sentence "God is one" depicts absolute truth, for the word "one" has an entirely different meaning when used in relation to God.[10]

What can we say about God? Nothing. We can say what God is not, and we can talk about God's creation and events that people felt were inspired by the divine. We cannot, however, meaningfully talk about God's essence or define God in any way, for to do so would be to confine God to a human concept. For Maimonides, the meaning of God's oneness is that God is beyond human thought, utterly transcendent and other. God is, and after that statement, we are left with silence. "To You, silence is praise" (Psalm 65:2).[11]

In the Divine Image

If we human beings do not have even a single characteristic in common with God, then what does the Torah mean that all human beings are made in the divine image (Genesis 1:27)? Surely, there must be something "God-like" about us that makes human beings special. It says so in the Torah.

Again, Maimonides explains, this is a metaphor. Maimonides understood the Torah to be a book of ideas and symbols, not a literal history of ancient people. In the Torah, human beings are singled out as the pinnacle of God's creative work. Human beings are special, Maimonides agrees, the culmination of six days of God's energy. This does not mean, however, that we share an attribute in common with God, either physically or emotionally. What it does mean is that the Torah draws a daring analogy: human beings are unique among the animal kingdom in a similar way that God is unique with respect to the universe.

To be in the divine image means to have something unique as a species that wholly sets us apart from all other living things, resembling how God is set apart from us. This is an analogy of difference. And the quality that makes human beings completely different from all animals is a gift that God gave us: a rational, moral conscience.

> The human species is unique in the world, without another species like it, in this respect, that one by one's own knowledge and reflection can know the difference between good and evil and can do what one desires.[12]

What makes human beings unique, Maimonides claims, is that human beings are the only species on earth that contemplates right and wrong. We are the only animal that deliberates about moral issues. Without our morality, our divine image is lost. We become animals just like all other creatures.

When we say the *Sh'ma*, therefore, we are not just affirming the uniqueness of God, that there is one Being that is transcendent to which nothing else can be compared. We are also affirming the uniqueness of humanity, that we are special because of the gift that God gave us in terms of our ability to reason and make moral decisions. Moreover, each and every human being is unique, unlike any other. This awareness that we are set apart in a fashion the way God is set apart is perhaps what it means to be holy.

Rabbi Akiba also reflected on the meaning of being made in the divine image and God's oneness. He said:

> Beloved are human beings, for they were created in the divine image. Even more beloved are they, because they can be aware of having been created in the divine image, as it is written, "For in the image of God, God made humanity" (Genesis 9:6).[13]

God is one, incomparable. And we human beings are also one, set apart from the rest of the earth. There is nothing like us in the entire world, for we are the creatures who care about God's moral authority, about our ethics. For Maimonides, the oneness of God, stripped of all pretense and fanciful imagery, is analogous to the oneness of humanity, stripped of its illusions and pretensions. Whether we like it or not, our uniqueness makes us responsible, one to the other.

"Hearing" Maimonides: Honoring Uniqueness

Moses Maimonides wrote different works for different audiences. His code of Jewish law, the *Mishneh Torah*, was meant for popular readership. In it he proposes a more straightforward faith, that one should pray to the one God and profess God's unity with the *Sh'ma*.

In the *Guide*, however, Maimonides wrote for the most advanced thinkers of his age. If those with great intellectual capacity and daring were to say the *Sh'ma*, Maimonides would not have them praying to a divine Person who had ears to hear. Nor would they be petitioning for God to grant a wish like an overgrown parent or a larger-than-life king. Rather, the philosophical elite in Maimonides's imagination would meditate on a principle, the knowledge that there is a completely transcendent Supreme Being that is the Source of the universe and our moral authority. In addition, they would contemplate the uniqueness of God and the uniqueness of humanity. Maimonides also probably imagined that this type of meditation was what Moses did on top of Mount Sinai when God "came down" to him, thinking and reflecting into a thunderous epiphany.

This kind of "stripped down" monotheism might be discomforting. To think of God in terms of a Principle or a Power is very different than to think of God as a Person. Yet the monotheism of Maimonides does, indeed, direct us to people, all of our fellow human beings. For Maimonides, monotheism was the greatest realization in the world, the complete uniqueness of God who is, nevertheless, our Creator. In order to truly appreciate this gift, we have to honor the uniqueness of God through the commandments and also honor the uniqueness in each other as moral beings.

This principle of the uniqueness of each human being can easily be lost, to not be "heard." We read in our newspapers of estimates of lives that are lost in disasters, and we have to round them off to the nearest zero. We can take our common humanity for granted and forget the moral responsibility we have for each other. Perhaps for this reason, the Talmud cautions us that when "one saves one life it is as if one has saved an entire world, and when one destroys one life it is as if one destroys an entire world."[14] The idea of the "one" is preserved in the *Sh'ma* to provoke our conscience.

Many Jews did not agree with Maimonides's ideas. It did not meet their emotional needs, especially in times of trauma. People needed a God who could literally hear them, who would protect them with loving arms. Rather than a God who was so transcendent as to be unreachable, they needed God to be close by in the here and now. More than they needed to hear God, they needed God to hear them. They were willing to tolerate a version of monotheism that was inconsistent if it gave them comfort. Maimonides changed the world with his ideas, and everyone had to take his understanding of one God seriously. But people could not live without their images. Jewish philosophy under Maimonides's guidance was too austere.

It is partly for this reason that Kabbalah, or Jewish mysticism, would become so wildly successful. In the aftermath of Christians conquering Muslim Spain and giving the Jews who lived there the choice to convert or die, Maimonides's intellectual contemplation was of little help. When the Jews of Spain were expelled in 1492, Jews did not just flee from the west to the east. They also fled from their heads to their hearts.

Hear O Israel,

שמע ישראל

YHVH is our God,

יי אלהינו

YHVH the Infinite One!

יי אחד

5

Communing with the One

Haim Vital

A Sacred Story

The student walked naked, his bare feet in the snow, toward the cave.

The earlier master had not asked for such severity, but the new one made such demands. When Rabbi Moses Cordovero headed the *chavurah,* or brotherhood, he was very strict with the disciples' behavior. No one ate any meat or drank any wine except on the Sabbath, and each was diligent with his prayers, concentrating on them with all of his attention. This particular disciple was especially dedicated. At the beginning of each of the four seasons, he fasted for three days, and he also fasted on the eve of every month before the New Moon. He could feel the sins of the Jewish people evaporate as he performed these actions, and the world was slowly being healed.

But the new master, the Ashkenazi Rabbi Isaac Luria,[1] demanded even more of him. The midnight vigils were longer and the fasts more extensive. And now, even in winter, he prepared to immerse himself in the ritual bath on this village mountaintop called Safed, just as the rabbi instructed.[2]

The pain of his feet in the snow and the wind on his body was so intense that it strangely felt like fire. He approached the cave and tried to push the pain out of his mind. Surely this agony was small when compared to the distress of God, whose earthly presence, the *Shechinah,* was writhing in exile.

The ritual bath was carved from the stone of the cave itself and was fed from the springs of the mountain. The free-flowing water made up a large enough quantity to be a vessel of purity as defined in the Talmud. A channel brought the water into the pool, and an underground opening took the water out, carrying away sin. Entering this water, all things were cleansed of impurities. Even the holy master himself used this particular ritual bath. Its power was such that no one could enter it without one day returning in repentance to God.

The disciple, named Haim Vital, stepped in front of the dark water and mentally recited the prayer to direct his intention to this holy act. He also prayed for loyalty to his new master, in whom he found renewed faith and trust. He could not say these meditations aloud, because his lips and cheeks would not move from the cold. With a sudden movement he jumped into the freezing water.

Hands pulled him out of the bath and wrapped a blanket around him. They carried him back to the building, where they laid him in front of the fire and dried him off. His brotherhood was extremely kind and loyal. Once he was warm enough to speak, they told him that he had lost consciousness.

"No," Haim Vital said. "For a moment I was united with the One."

They nodded approvingly. Thus was the mystery of such an immersion. By returning to the primordial waters, a person also went back in time; as if a fetus in the womb of God, the mind disappeared into the Infinite. As Haim Vital's limbs came back to life, he promised to write down every one of the holy rabbi's words, for his experience had affirmed the master's wisdom. He pledged to be Rabbi Luria's foremost disciple.

Later, Haim Vital was dressed in his finest clothes, and he was once again warm. He looked forward to being with his wife and children for the Sabbath dinner. Before doing so, he gathered with the members of his brotherhood, and they welcomed the Sabbath Queen together. The Sabbath was a special time when the *Shechinah,* the feminine aspect of God, would be united with the Holy One, Blessed Be He, God's masculine side. They sang out a

hymn composed by an earlier master of their village, Rabbi
Solomon Alkabetz the Levite, greeting the Bride and encouraging
her in her union. It was through this union of the masculine and
the feminine that the world would be healed:

> *L'cha dodi likrat kalah p'nei Shabbat n'kabbalah!*
>> Come, my Beloved, to meet the Bride; let us welcome
> the face of the Sabbath!
>> ... YHVH is one, and God's Name is one, for honor,
> for glory, and for praise![3]

Then they joined in prayers. After reciting a blessing over the mystery of Creation, they all took a deep breath together. They tried
to purify their thoughts. In this holy moment, they intoned the
Sh'ma, using one breath for each word. While doing so, they kept
in mind the explanation of their beloved teacher Rabbi Moses
Cordovero, of blessed memory:

> Everything is within it [the Infinite]; it is within everything
> and outside of everything. There is nothing but it.[4]
>> "Hear O Israel, YHVH is our God, YHVH the Infinite
> One!"

Exile and Redemption

How did the Jews of Safed, living such an unusually ascetic lifestyle,
come to be there? In order to understand their lives and their
thoughts behind the *Sh'ma,* we have to understand their history,
going back a century and a half.

When King Ferdinand and Queen Isabella of Spain expelled
the Jews of their country in 1492, they destroyed a community that
had existed for centuries. It created a trauma for the Jewish community second only to the destruction of the Temple in Jerusalem.

The expulsion, however, did not happen all at once. Tension
between Jews and Christians began at the start of the Reconquista,
and by the mid-thirteenth century, Christians effectively controlled

the Iberian Peninsula. Once Christians had conquered Spain, the overall position of comfort the Jews had enjoyed there disappeared. Jews were considered the enemies of Jesus who had put him on the cross. This new reality put them in constant physical danger as violent anti-Semitism was encouraged by the state, but there was a spiritual challenge as well. The Jewish community faced the full force of Christian proselytizing. In many communities, Jews were given the choice to convert or die, and many chose to be Conversos, or, according to the more common derogatory term given to them by their neighbors, Marranos, meaning "pigs." These Jews often practiced Christianity in public while secretly keeping their sacred Jewish traditions in the home. The Jewish encounter with Christianity in Spain was filled with peril.

From this environment, a new kind of Jewish mysticism was born. At the end of the thirteenth century, a new commentary on the Torah appeared bearing the name *Zohar*. It was filled with strange poetry and imagery that captured the imagination of the Jewish community and gave them many of the answers they sought in their difficult situation.

Once the Jews were expelled from Spain in 1492, this new mysticism became much more widespread among the Jewish refugees. The exiles were welcomed by the Ottoman Empire in the East, which valued their banking and trading skills. At the beginning of the sixteenth century, the Ottomans expanded their rule to include the Land of Israel, and Jews were allowed to move back to their ancestral homeland. The *Zohar* came with them, and the study of Kabbalah, or Jewish mysticism, became a powerful force in circles of Jewish learning.

A community formed in a town called Safed in the very north of the Land of Israel. It was more prosperous than Jerusalem because of its proximity to the Syrian Jewish community in Aleppo and its strong textile trade. Here many Jewish scholars gathered, drawn also by the chance to be near the graves of some of the famous sages of antiquity. They founded a strong community of Talmud study and Jewish law, including the scholarship of Rabbi

Joseph Karo, who penned the *Shulchan Aruch,* the authoritative code of Jewish law that stands at the heart of traditional Judaism to this day. Safed was most famous, however, for being a center of Kabbalah and commentary on the *Zohar.*

The kabbalists may have found a new home, but they carried with them the scars of the expulsion from Spain. They contemplated when the Messiah might appear, for surely the kind of death and pain they had seen could only be a sign of the end of days. These men formed brotherhoods and took upon themselves an ascetic lifestyle to purify themselves in readiness. They instituted new rituals, such as midnight vigils and fasts, and they authored new prayers to increase their devotion to God. Symbolically they wept for the destruction of the Temple in Jerusalem, but underneath their tears was a cry of pain from the trauma of the last century. Everything felt fragmentary and broken, and the kabbalists sought wholeness and peace with God.

Some of the most famous kabbalists composed the most radical and daring of Jewish theologies. Rabbi Moses Cordovero (1522–1570) systematized the teachings and commentaries on the *Zohar,* and he explained that God was to be understood as one and beyond all comprehension. At the same time, however, God was said to have created the world through exactly ten emanations of light. The doctrine of the ten *sefirot,* or aspects of God, became a common understanding of reality in Safed. For the kabbalists, the ten *sefirot* were the ten dimensions of the universe, as accepted as gravity or magnetism is today. Yet these dimensions were also supposed to carry with them aspects of the divine, such as compassion, majesty, and wisdom. Whereas Maimonides and previous thinkers sought to strip away anthropomorphisms, the kabbalists heaped such embodiments of the divine one on top of the other in an infinite variety. Ironically, just as Maimonides sought to harmonize Judaism with Hellenistic philosophy available in his environment, the kabbalists sought to reconcile their faith with their Gnostic and Christian milieu.

When Rabbi Moses Cordovero died in 1570, a new, even more radical teacher arose. While he led the community for only two years, his impact was far greater. Rabbi Isaac Luria (1534–1572), later known as the Ari or "Lion" (taking the first letters of the Hebrew words *Elohi Rav Yitzchak,* meaning the "Holy Rabbi Isaac"), led an extremely ascetic lifestyle and demanded the same of his disciples. He recounted even more poetic and imaginative stories of the divine than had previous teachers. Rabbi Haim Vital (1542–1620) became his foremost disciple, and he wrote down and spread the teachings of Rabbi Isaac Luria, meditating on every word.

Under these teachers, the meaning of the *Sh'ma* changed dramatically. Rather than proclaiming one simple, incomprehensible Supreme Being, the kabbalists understood God to be the culmination of an infinite number of powers and archetypes, including a king, a queen, light, darkness, the heavenly, and the demonic. God was beyond all things and yet manifest everywhere. The kabbalists did not care if their images contradicted each other or if their teachings were irrational. Their world was irrational, and their God was above reason. God contained and yet transcended the world, and so the highest name for God that they proclaimed was *Ein Sof,* or the One Without End.

For the kabbalists, the *Echad* of the *Sh'ma* meant that God was the Infinite One. This kind of thinking also opened up infinite possibilities in the Jewish community's imagination. In the kabbalist's heart, through meditation, prayer, and deed, the deepest desire was to commune with the One, to obliterate the self and disappear into the ultimate unity that was God.

Tiferet and *Shechinah*

Moses Maimonides and others had gone to great lengths to point out that God was above human characteristics and emotions. The kabbalists, however, took a completely different approach. Instead of God being beyond everything, God was all-encompassing. God was manifest in everything and everyone. God was part of the world and yet also rose above it.[5]

The world, however, was in chaos. The kabbalists felt that this meant God, too, experienced the trauma that they felt. As the world was a part of God, so was the world's pain. In fact, it was the disunity of the world created by human sin that caused the ten *sefirot* to be out of sync with each other. The world lacked harmony, and it was up to the mystic to try to bring balance back to the universe and back to God.

This metaphor of the world, and through the world the divine, needing to be realigned was especially prevalent with regard to gender. Rather than God being beyond gender, the kabbalists understood that God was both male and female and yet also somehow transcended them. God, therefore, had both a male and a female side, while still being infinite.

The kabbalists recognized that male and female, like all things, were at odds with each other, and so it must be with God. One of the central dramas of Kabbalah was to unite the masculine with the feminine and bring wholeness to the universe. Through ritual, prayer, and study, the kabbalists felt they could bring the masculine and feminine aspects of God together that were currently experiencing exile. Two of the ten *sefirot* were designated as representing God's male and female sides. The masculine they called *Tiferet,* meaning "beauty," and the female they called *Shechinah,* meaning "presence."

When the kabbalists said prayers on the Sabbath, they felt they were encouraging the union of *Tiferet* and *Shechinah* and thus bringing wholeness to the masculine and the feminine in the universe and in God. When they sang the hymn *L'cha Dodi,* they were greeting "the Sabbath Queen," representing *Shechinah,* and encouraging her to enter into the bridal canopy of "the Beloved," standing for *Tiferet.* This imagery was also understood to pertain to the *Sh'ma.* The *Zohar* reads:

> When Israel engages in the mystical unification of the
> *Sh'ma* with a perfect will, a light emerges from the secret of
> the supernal world.... All the trees in the Garden of Eden
> exhale perfumes and praise their Master, for then the con-
> sort is adorned for entry into the canopy with her hus-
> band.... Therefore we arouse her and say: "Hear, O Israel":
> Prepare yourself. Your husband comes to you in all his fin-
> ery, and is ready to meet you. "YHVH, our God, YHVH" is a
> single unification, with a single will, without any separa-
> tion.... Then the consort prepares herself and adorns
> herself, and her ministers bring her to her husband, whis-
> pering in a soft voice, "Blessed is God's glorious majesty for
> ever and ever." This is said in a whisper, for this is the cor-
> rect way to bring her to her husband. Happy are the people
> who know this and who order this celestial arrangement
> of faith![6]

According to the *Zohar,* the proclamation of the *Sh'ma* is about the
unification of the masculine and feminine aspects of God. The
people Israel who say this prayer are in effect announcing and urg-
ing the wedding union of these two sides of the divine. As they did
this, they also felt that they were healing their world, bringing the
duality of male versus female to a harmonious resolution.

The *Zohar* also goes out of its way to state that "YHVH, our
God, YHVH is a single unification, with a single will, without any
separation." This statement reveals another part of the kabbalists'
agenda, which was responding to the Christian polemics that they
had endured. It was well known at the time that Christians believed
that Deuteronomy mentioned God three times in this statement
(YHVH, our God, YHVH) because this revealed the Trinity. In
reaction to this, the kabbalists made sure to explain that this was
entirely about the unity of God, "without any separation."[7]

It may seem strange to us that the kabbalists would divide
God's aspects up into ten *sefirot* as well as masculine and feminine
and then be adamant about the rejection of God being three. The

kabbalists understood, however, that they were speaking in metaphors about reality as they knew it, whereas the Trinity was a Christian doctrine about salvation through Jesus, a doctrine they, of course, rejected. To the mystics, these were wholly different ideas. The ten *sefirot* were a description of the dimensions of the universe, and the universe in all of its diversity was a manifestation of God. To see everything as part of a larger, infinite whole was the ultimate aim. Through meditating on the *Sh'ma,* the mystics tried to raise themselves up to this higher, more enlightened level of awareness.

In this spirit, the *Zohar* is content to contradict itself by providing an alternative understanding of the *Sh'ma* in a different passage, so long as it leads to the idea of the unification of the universe. According to this other passage, the six words of the *Sh'ma* correspond to the six directions of space: north, south, east, west, up, and down. All of space, therefore, is united with this phrase. Similarly, the proclamation that is said after the *Sh'ma* in the prayer service also has six words: *Baruch shem kavod malchuto l'olam va'ed.* ("Blessed is God's glorious majesty for ever and ever.") These proclamations are said during prayer consecutively. The kabbalists understood this to mean that just as all space is united from all six directions in the heavenly realm with the first statement, so are they united on earth with the following statement as the people Israel say this prayer.[8]

It Is All God: Working Within the Divine

When the kabbalists of Safed said the *Sh'ma,* they felt that they were revealing the unity of the cosmos, uniting all duality and resolving all contradictions. They understood themselves as well as all things as manifestations of the divine. Rabbi Moses Cordovero wrote: "Do not say, 'This is a stone and not God.' God forbid! Rather, all existence is God, and the stone is a thing pervaded by divinity."[9] For the kabbalists, God was immanent, available in every place at every moment. There was not anything in which God was not present. Rather than thinking of God as purely transcendent above them, the kabbalists emphasized how close by God was in their lives, an almost tangible reality.

From this point of view, the kabbalists felt human beings were in a privileged position to realize that they were working within the realm of the divine. There was great power but also great humility in the knowledge that one is a part of God, but so is everything else. Therefore, every deed had its consequences. Every sin causes damage to others, to the world, and to God, and every divine commandment and good deed mends something that is broken.

The kabbalists preached that it is the duty of every person to seek *tikkun olam,* the repair of the world. By practicing God's commandments with faithful intentions, a person could help to heal the cosmos. Rabbi Isaac Luria formulated this doctrine in a radical and picturesque way: There are divine sparks hidden in all things. When we bring goodness into the world and obey God's will, we release these sparks and raise them up to heaven.[10]

The kabbalists therefore demanded that all people consider their deeds carefully. They were especially disciplined with themselves in the pursuit of what they thought was the divine path, purifying themselves with fasting and prayer. They weighed every act and every word. At the same time, however, they also knew that God was their partner, empowering them to confront the problems of the world. As part of the divine pattern, they believed they could achieve unity as human beings with the universe.

"Hearing" the Kabbalists: The Repair of the World

The kabbalists sought to repair their world. They sought inner healing and wholeness after a century of trauma. Though much of their imagery and teaching may be completely foreign to the modern world, we can still empathize with their feelings and desires.

By saying the *Sh'ma,* the kabbalists tried to bring unity to all things that normally would be thought of as conflicting, such as

male and female or love and judgment. They felt that they were a
small part of the Infinite and actors in a divine drama. They craved
communion with the One as a result of their spiritual discipline.

They also understood that to be a partner with God meant a
great responsibility. Perhaps we can understand their worldview
from this Rabbinic parable: Imagine that all of the world's deeds
are on a scale, divided up into good deeds and sins. At the present
moment, all of the sins on one side of the scale are equally bal-
anced against all of the world's acts of goodness. The next deed
that you do will tip the scale in one direction or the other.
What you do has great consequences for you, for the world, and
for God.[11]

The kabbalists felt enormous responsibility for the world
around them. To hear the *Sh'ma* through their voice today means
to become seekers of unity. Perhaps we might also see ourselves as
partners with God in healing the world.

שמע ישראל

Hear O Israel,

יי אלהינו

YHVH our God

יי אחד

is YHVH the one ruler!

"Master of the Universe"

Moses Haim Luzzatto

A Sacred Story

The Jewish merchant stepped into the shop in Amsterdam, leaving the two bodyguards in the damp air outside. He always walked with bodyguards now, each one armed with a large wooden club and a small pistol. In his breast pocket, he carried a pouch of uncut diamonds. People had to be careful whenever they were on the road.

The merchant reached up and removed the mask that was over his nose and mouth. The plague was still strong, and in addition to fearing robbers, he also was cautious about disease. What demons had brought such dangers to his life?

The inside of the small shop was brightly lit with lanterns. The work of polishing diamonds required a great deal of illumination, but although all the lamps were burning, no one was to be found. "Hello?" the merchant called. "Rabbi Moses?"

The rabbi who worked in the shop was recently from Italy. He had come to Amsterdam under difficult circumstances. He was famous for being a prodigy at Talmud, but he had become even more famous for his practice of Kabbalah, of Jewish mysticism. Rumor had it that even though his genius was widely recognized, the rabbi had strayed into the realm of magic. The rabbi's home in Padua had been searched, and the community leaders found what they claimed was incriminating evidence. The local rabbis ostracized him and forbade him from teaching Kabbalah any more.

Eventually, the famous scholar had to move. He came to Amsterdam, and he took up polishing diamonds in order to support himself. The rabbi's name was Moses Haim Luzzatto.

The merchant took out the pouch and tentatively stepped deeper into the store. He ducked his head past the lanterns and walked toward the back room. Slowly pushing back the curtain that divided the two chambers, the merchant called out again, "Rabbi Moses?"

Unlike the first room, this one was dimly lit. The rabbi was seated in a chair in front of one candle. In his hand he held up a diamond, cut and polished. The rabbi seemed to be staring into it. It seemed as if he had not heard the merchant's calls, as if the rabbi were in a trance. His pupils were dilated as he stared, unblinking, into the diamond's facets.

"Facets of one diamond," the rabbi muttered. "Unity. One pattern. One design."

"Rabbi Moses?" the merchant tried once more in a whisper.

"Yes," the rabbi continued, hearing yet not hearing, not looking in the man's direction. "Yes. I am Moses. Moses our teacher."

The merchant stood completely still, wondering. Could the rabbi have meant ... ?

Suddenly the rabbi turned toward him, closing his fist around the diamond he was holding. "Reuben!" he said. "How are you?" It was quickly business as usual.

The merchant dropped off the merchandise and set a date by which the work was to be completed. By the time he returned to his bodyguards waiting for him outside, it was as if the scene he had interrupted never took place. He boarded his carriage and took off down the road. He decided he would not mention it to anyone. No one needed another scandal.[1]

Anticipating the Messiah

Rabbi Moses Haim Luzzatto (1707–1746) was one of the most outstanding scholars of his generation. He lived at the end of the

Middle Ages and the beginning of the modern era, and his writing is a reflection of this transitional time. From his own perspective, however, he felt that he was living at the end of time, approaching the appearance of the Messiah.

Raised in Italy, Luzzatto received the education of a well-to-do family. Anticipating modern studies, Luzzatto studied not only Talmud and Bible but also science, poetry, and literature. He became proficient in all areas and even composed hymns and dramas for his friends at their weddings.

In the year 1727, however, Luzzatto underwent a life-altering experience. While studying Kabbalah, he suddenly heard a heavenly voice, a muse that mystics termed in Hebrew a *maggid*. He began to write down the revelations of the voice inside his head, and he gathered a group of scholars around him to study mysticism together. This group decided that it was within their power to bring the Messiah in their own day. They met in secret to perform rites of their own devising, believing passionately that God's messenger was about to appear to perfect the world, largely because of their efforts.

When the group was discovered by the authorities of the Jewish community, it was broken up, and the members were put under a ban from practicing these messianic speculations. While today many might think that such preoccupation with the Messiah is primarily a Christian activity, in the Middle Ages it was a large part of the Jewish world as well. Luzzatto's efforts might have been deemed heresy, but they were not unusual. The plague was killing thousands, and many thought that the end must be near.

Luzzatto agreed to the ban on his kabbalistic teachings. When he married, however, some began to wonder. Luzzatto's first name was Moses, and his marriage to a woman named Zipporah mirrored the life of Moses in the Torah. The biblical Moses had also married a woman named Zipporah, and some thought Luzzatto was purposefully imitating the biblical Moses's life. The truth was even more provocative. From his letters, it can be deduced that Moses Haim Luzzatto believed he was actually the reincarnation of the original Moses. While belief in reincarnation was not part of the mainstream among Jewish people, it was not completely rejected either. Luzzatto's contemporaries could not tolerate his audaciousness that he would claim to have the same soul as Moses himself. They harassed him until he moved to Amsterdam. In Venice, his books were banned and destroyed.

It was in Amsterdam, however, that Luzzatto wrote his most enduring works. History would forgive his heretical leanings. In addition to his kabbalistic writings, he also wrote systematic treatises on ethics and Jewish beliefs, which became standard reading in the yeshivas of eastern Europe. Some even required that their students memorize his most famous book, *The Path of the Upright*. His poetry and dramas in Hebrew also anticipated the work of Enlightenment thinkers and modern Hebrew poetry. With his Old World beliefs but contemporary style, Luzzatto was truly a man who lived between two time periods.

In one of his most popular books, *The Way of God*, Luzzatto discussed at length the importance of the *Sh'ma*. For Luzzatto, understanding God's unity was the key to bringing about God's perfection of the world. It was central to any understanding of Judaism. Luzzatto believed that if Jews would say the *Sh'ma* with complete devotion, they could, through their own efforts, cause God to send the Messiah. It was this kind of activity that caused him so much trouble.

Luzzatto did not stay in Amsterdam. He traveled to the Land of Israel, where he thought he could teach and study Kabbalah without hindrance. Very shortly after his arrival, he died of the plague at age thirty-nine.[2]

Divine Sovereignty

Luzzatto summarizes his discussion on the *Sh'ma* by stating that reciting the *Sh'ma* means to declare that God is the sole Master of the universe. God is not just a Ruler who gives commandments to people to be obeyed. God also rules over the laws of nature.

Human beings and the elements are both subject to God's will. For Luzzatto, God is Sovereign over the world above, full of angels and heavenly bodies, as well as below, among forests, fields, and peoples.[3] One God means one ultimate ruling power and authority over all of creation.

The notion of God as Sovereign Ruler over the universe is as old as the Bible. The Psalms are full of statements declaring that God has dominion over the heavens and the earth and that nature conforms to God's commands. The Psalmist understood God's rule over the forces of nature to be full of joy and praise.

> Praise YHVH, O you who are on earth,
> all sea monsters and ocean depths,
> fire and hail, snow and smoke,
> storm wind that executes God's command,
> all mountains and hills,
> all fruit trees and cedars,
> all wild and tamed beasts,
> creeping things and winged birds,
> all kings and peoples of the earth,
> all princes of the earth and its judges,
> youths and maidens alike,
> old and young together. (Psalm 148:7–12)

The storm wind obeys God's commands the same way the kings do. God's rule, whether over oceans, trees, or nations, was considered joyful and just.

In this spirit, Luzzatto used innovative terms to refer to God. He referred to God as the Authority,[4] and by doing so, he meant that not only human beings turn to God's rule, but also the elements.

> God gave the elements of creation the ability to rule over their own particular domains, and each one can accomplish many things, according to its particular nature. In reality, however, none of these things has any power or authority other than that given to it by God. The only One

who is the true all-powerful Ruler and Authority is God Himself.[5]

A second name for God that Luzzatto employs is Highest Wisdom.[6] In doing so, Luzzatto calls to mind a mystical notion of a light shining from above that gradually dissipates into darkness. The Highest Wisdom is the source of divine illumination, but as it descends toward the physical realm that we inhabit, blurriness and obscurity become thicker and deeper. This gradual darkening, however, is part of God's will and the stage upon which human beings are created and enabled to act. Only spiritual beings can endure the brightness from above.[7]

Luzzatto did not confine himself to this top-down metaphor. In the very same essay, he also reversed the imagery with a third unusual term, God as the Root.[8] This is also borrowed from Kabbalah, and it is used as a metaphor for the Cause or Reason behind things. The same way that a root grows upward into a stem of a plant and then continues to differentiate itself into leaves, flowers, and fruit, so too do the causes and effects of creation branch out through the universe. The variety of nature and life is a result of God's will:

> We must realize that God willed many types of entities into existence. These include entities above and below, spiritual and physical, all arranged by God in various different ways.... The Root and Cause of all these things, however, is God alone.[9]

For Luzzatto, the diversity and beautiful variety of the world are the artistic expression of God. Each creation has a place and purpose, and every thing goes back to the same origin. Every creature is like a flower on a tree that shares the same Root.

A fourth and final unusual term Luzzatto uses for God in the context of God's oneness is Director.[10] For Luzzatto, God as Ruler meant more than recognizing God as the Supreme Force over nature. "God is ... actually the Director of all things, and His plan alone is what will abide."[11] For Luzzatto, God has an ongoing relationship with the world. God does not rule from afar, uninvolved like oblivious royalty locked in a tower. God directs the world's events and responds to our lives. Luzzatto understands the *Sh'ma* to be an affirmation of God's existence, authority, and providence.[12]

Luzzatto felt that all of these different understandings of God are implicit in the idea of God being one. The final term, however, that of God being Director, begs a question: If God is the sole Director of all things, ordering them just so, then why does the world seem to be so chaotic?

A Wild Thicket or a Well-Arranged Garden?

Luzzatto admits that the world may seem devoid of purpose. The universe seems like a random place. More than that, life is full of misfortune that is undeserved. If God is the Director of all things, how can such calamities be allowed to occur? If God has a plan, it is not discernible to the human mind. In spite of these admissions, however, Luzzatto insists that, though God's ultimate pattern to the universe is incomprehensible, nevertheless a plan exists. Luzzatto believes that God is the Cause of all things and gives the world purpose.

> Even though things may come about through many exceedingly complex and roundabout ways, all this originates from God, who is bringing everything to its ultimate goal of true perfection. Even though this might not be obvious now, it is the ultimate underlying truth, and it will be revealed and known in the end.[13]

Luzzatto thinks of the chaos in the world as the "roundabout ways" of God. What does not make sense to the human mind is simply a function of its limitation to discern a divine purpose. Ultimately, there is order and meaning to the universe, even if we may never grasp it fully.

Even evil, according to Luzzatto, has a role to play in God's world. Unlike other religions in which evil has its own independent existence, monotheism has only one God as the origin of all. This idea, too, also originates from the Bible. Through the prophet Isaiah, God says, "I am YHVH and there is none else. I form light and create darkness, I make peace and create evil. I am YHVH, and I do all these things" (Isaiah 45:6–7).

Luzzatto also believed that all things, good and bad, are a part of God's ultimate design. The *Sh'ma* proclaims that there is only one God, and Luzzatto is willing to confront monotheism with chaos and evil in the world. Evil is a reality that cannot be ignored, nor can its existence be blamed upon another power in the universe. All things come from God. Luzzatto resolves this problem by reiterating God's goodness and claiming that all things will ultimately serve a good end. When this greater good is achieved, things that are currently regarded as evil will be revealed for being necessary tools God employed.

What we human beings are witnessing, therefore, is the middle of a process, an unfinished trajectory. The pattern of the world and of history is not complete. We cannot discern the order and meaning of the universe because we are in a plan that has not been fulfilled. Luzzatto understands the "one point, the perfection of creation" is not yet. We are moving forward in time. Our perspective is limited from our one vantage point at a particular moment and place. God, who is eternal, is not constrained by such limitations. Ultimately, the "roundabout ways" of God will redeem the world. There is order behind the chaos, even if we cannot see it.

Luzzatto employs a metaphor in the introduction to *Way of God* that reveals his understanding of the universe. In laying out his program for the book, he differentiates between the person who knows the subject at hand versus the person who is just beginning to study. This applies to all fields: When we are beginning to learn something, many things seem random and chaotic. As we progress, we begin to see the interrelationships among the various elements. He illustrates by saying:

> It is very much like the difference between looking at a well-
> arranged garden, planted in rows and patterns, and seeing
> a wild thicket or forest growing in confusion.[14]

We can all look at the same group of plants. Whether one sees a well-arranged garden or a wild thicket does not depend on how the plants are actually growing. It depends entirely on the experience of the viewer. An inexperienced person cannot see a pattern, but the person with more wisdom can. Similarly, the universe, which might seem like a wild forest to us human beings, is to God a beautifully designed garden.

The Ultimate True Perfection: One End

Luzzatto understood the universe to be a well-ordered place, even if it could not be comprehended by human beings. The pattern of the universe was moving toward a sense of ultimate fulfillment. This time of "the ultimate goal of true perfection"[15] is the coming of the Messiah, a descendent of King David. According to Luzzatto, the world will be transformed by the Messiah, and everything will make sense at last.[16]

Human beings, and especially Jews, are not powerless in waiting for this time of redemption to come. Luzzatto does not see us as mere bystanders in this divine drama. He certainly did not see himself that way, as he personally performed rites and prayers that he thought would help hasten the Messiah's coming. It was for this activity that he was cast out of his community in Italy.

Nevertheless, it is interesting to note that Luzzatto felt all Jewish people could have a role in bringing about the Messianic Age. One of the chief tools that the people Israel could use to bring about this time was the daily recitation of the *Sh'ma*. Luzzatto believed that when Jews declare monotheism to the world, God releases greater illumination and goodness upon creation.

> When the Jew bears witness to God's unity ... then God
> reciprocates and responds in a similar manner. God exalts

himself in his unity and strengthens it, thus enhancing the rectification of the world. This proceeds step by step, through all the roundabout ways of this world, leading to the ultimate true rectification. God's plan is then fulfilled.[17]

The Jewish people's actions in the world below are reciprocated by God from above. Luzzatto believed that when Jews declare that God is one through the *Sh'ma,* God makes the world more whole. The one goal of the pattern of creation draws nearer.

We accomplish this when we recite the *Sh'ma.* When one does this, it causes sanctity and enlightenment to be transmitted to all creation, raising it by some degree from the worldly darkness that exists in its fundamental level.[18]

Declaring the *Sh'ma* has cosmic importance for Luzzatto. His hope is that ultimately, all humankind will follow the Jewish people's example and also declare God's unity. In doing so, the one God of Israel will bring fulfillment to a united humanity.

"Hearing" Luzzatto: A Theory of Everything?

Rabbi Moses Haim Luzzatto, while ostracized in his own day, has come to represent contemporary Orthodox Jewish theology. His works are still studied and memorized in yeshivas to this day. For Luzzatto, his recital of the *Sh'ma* was an act of faith: faith in the order and purpose of the universe, faith in the coming of the Messianic Age, and faith in his personal role to actively and meaningfully contribute to that end.

Many modern people today have a difficult time taking such beliefs on faith. We skeptics rebel against the idea of a personal Messiah, one figure who comes to bring peace, justice, and compassion to the whole world. We also have trouble believing that simply by saying the words of the *Sh'ma,* we directly affect history and the order of the universe. Such beliefs might strike us as a form of magic, which Luzzatto was accused of practicing.

Before we dismiss such a theology, however, we ought to take seriously the question that lies at the heart of Luzzatto's belief: Does God have a plan for us? Do we believe the world is simply a chaotic, random place? Or is there some order, and perhaps some sense of fulfillment, awaiting future generations?

To illustrate what it means to "hear" Luzzatto's understanding of the *Sh'ma*, we can look to someone who might be seen as standing on the opposite side of the spectrum from the kabbalist.

Albert Einstein was a scientist who did not believe in the Messiah, nor a personal God, nor in divine reward and punishment. He did, however, marvel in wonder at the universe that he felt was a manifestation of God. He felt that "the most beautiful and most profound emotion we can experience is the sensation of the mystical. It is the sower of all true science."[19] And it was Einstein who believed that a deeper reality existed underneath what we experience as separate forces, implying a sense of harmony to the universe.

During the last twenty-five years of his life, Einstein worked on a unified field theory, a theory that would unite his understanding of relativity with his quantum theory. In short, he was seeking one scientific statement that would explain everything. It was "intolerable" to him that gravitational and electromagnetic forces could be independent of each other.[20] Rather, for Einstein, the scientist should strive to bring together all concepts and consolidate all diversity back to an undifferentiated unity. Is this not similar to Luzzatto's goal of understanding the mystical unity of all creation under God's dominion?

Einstein did not succeed in perfecting a unified field theory. He died with this labor unfinished. Nevertheless, we might ask what relationship such a theory of everything might have to the *Sh'ma*, and what relationship that in turn might have to traditional Jewish belief.[21]

For both Einstein and Luzzatto, the world was a "well-arranged garden" and not a "wild thicket," even if human beings could not quite comprehend how it all came together. They understood that the world was not left to chance. "God is one" means that there is one Ruler of the universe, even if we might disagree about how that rule is carried out.

Can we, too, see ourselves as a part of some larger pattern of meaning? Do our actions count, in the larger scheme of things, as one infinitesimal part of the universe? Are we a part of God's purpose?

Hear O people and Land of Israel,

שמע ישראל

YHVH is our God,

יי אלהינו

YHVH unites us!

יי אחד

A Nation Reborn

Abraham Isaac Kook

A Sacred Story

Right foot behind the left, left stepping out, arm linked in arm. The dancers formed a circle as they sang. They danced the hora, a circle-dance from eastern Europe, going faster and faster. The symbol of the circle represented unity, and the faster it went, the more ecstatic they felt.

Night had descended, and the fire illuminated all of their faces. The Zionist pioneers celebrated their work in the Land of Israel. It was the dawn of the twentieth century. They had come to transform the wilderness into an inhabitable community, but they had also come to be transformed themselves. They had been "ghetto Jews," targets of pogroms. Now they were standing on their own soil, their ancient homeland, full of pride as they built the foundation of a nation.

Most of the Zionist pioneers had dropped their Yiddish names. Instead, they took on Hebrew names, and with them a new identity. They had also dropped the trappings of eastern Europe; instead of long black coats, beards for men, and covered hair for women, they stood in work clothes with shorts and sandals. They had also left behind religion. Their new expression of Judaism was a secular national identity.

One face in the dancing circle stood out as different from the others. He had kept his beard and mustache, and he still dressed in the traditional garb of Ashkenazi Judaism. A fur hat adorned his head. He was also deeply religious, fulfilling Jewish law strictly in his everyday practice. Rabbi Abraham Isaac Kook was a new breed: a religious Zionist. A passionate mystic and Orthodox in his belief and behavior, he nevertheless spoke fluent Hebrew for everyday conversation, something that his more traditional colleagues considered heresy. He was also passionate about rebuilding the Land of Israel, and he encouraged the pioneers. In his mind, it was not enough to wait for the Messiah to come to bring Jews to the Land of Israel, as many of the other rabbis thought. Kook understood that the Jewish people could not wait and needed to take action themselves. In Kook's view, the Zionist secular pioneers, whether they knew it or not, were serving God's purpose. He danced with them in the circle, and they accepted him. He was a curiosity to them, or perhaps something more.

The hora ended, and people slowly drifted back to their homes. These houses were makeshift buildings. Malaria was common, and much of the work consisted of planting eucalyptus trees to drain the swamps. Even though the rabbi was different, they appreciated his coming. They knew that simply by associating himself with them, Kook angered many of his colleagues.

As Kook took to his bed, he uttered his nightly recitation of the *Sh'ma*. As he did so, his mind meditated on unification: the mystical unification of God and this world, and the bringing together of one nation in an act of redemption. In his mind, the oneness of God was inseparably linked with the unity of the people Israel. He would do his best to build connections between the religious and the secular, for the Jewish return to the Land of Israel was the beginning of a new era for Judaism and for the world. God, Torah, and Israel would draw closer together than ever before.

Pioneering Religious Zionist

Rabbi Abraham Isaac Kook (1865–1935) was the first Ashkenazi chief rabbi of Palestine before the founding of the State of Israel.

He was born in northwestern Russia and was educated at the academy in Volozhin, the largest yeshiva of its time with almost five hundred students. It was at this yeshiva, receiving a traditional education in Talmud and Jewish law, that Kook began speaking Hebrew as an everyday language. This was a very unpopular thing to do, as religious Jews felt Hebrew should be reserved for prayer and study. In addition, Kook undertook other nontraditional practices, such as the study of modern philosophy. Most of all, he became a devoted Zionist, committed to the restoration of a Jewish home in the Land of Israel.

Kook defied categorization. The earliest Zionists were secular, people who embraced nationalism as the solution to responding to anti-Semitism and answering the Jewish people's distress. In doing so, they left religion behind as part of a previous life. While there were some religious groups that had begun organizing and settling in the Land of Israel prior to Kook's time, they had no conception of Jewish statehood. The first Zionist immigration, consisting of people who came to found and sustain a Jewish state in the historic Jewish homeland, was overwhelmingly secular in nature. Opposed to these earliest Zionists were Orthodox Jews who believed that only God should act to bring Jews to the Holy Land with the coming of the Messiah. To try to "hasten the coming of the Messiah" by fighting for a country was deemed a sin. Still another faction, liberal Jews who were products of the Enlightenment, also opposed Zionism, for they argued that being Jewish was merely their religion and that they were wholeheartedly patriots of their country of origin, such as Germany or Russia.

Kook felt he could be a modern thinker, Orthodox, and a Zionist all at the same time. After serving as a rabbi in eastern Europe, he moved to the Land of Israel and became the rabbi of the city of Jaffa. He challenged both secular and religious Jews; in his version of Zionism, Jews could not fully be Jewish unless they lived in the Holy Land and lived by the Torah simultaneously.

While in Israel, Kook continued to do what was unpopular but true to his vision of the future of Judaism. He remained strictly

Orthodox, yet he was also on friendly terms with all of the secular
Zionist pioneers who worked the land. He also interpreted Jewish
law leniently so as to enable these pioneers to farm during the sab-
batical year, a year that, according to the Torah, the land was supposed to lie fallow. He did so by constructing a fictitious bill of sale
for plots of land to non-Jews. In this way, the land would symbolically be owned by people who were not Jewish for a nominal price,
and the pioneers could work the land in order to survive. Upon
the completion of the year, the pioneers "bought" back the land
that they truly owned. Such leniency antagonized Kook's
Orthodox colleagues, but he felt this was the true interpretation of
God's will.

Kook found himself in England during World War I and
unable to return to Palestine. He used his time of exile to actively
campaign for a Jewish state. Partly due to his efforts, the Balfour
Declaration, recognizing Israel as a Jewish national homeland, was
delivered by the British in 1917. With the completion of the war,
he was invited back by the Jewish community in Jerusalem to be
the first Ashkenazi chief rabbi of Israel. Throughout his time,
Kook was a symbol of the unity of the Jewish people, and he built
bridges between the different factions of the Jewish community.[1]

In addition to being an important political figure, Rabbi
Abraham Isaac Kook was also a mystic. His longing for the unity of
the Jewish people, especially while in the Land of Israel, was also a
longing for union with God. He wrote many kabbalistic essays and
poems. His love of the Jewish people, his Zionism, and his desire
for God were inseparable. He refused to be defined by his time
period's conventions.

A Double-Edged Sword: The Physical and the Spiritual

Rabbi Abraham Isaac Kook wrote essays, legal decisions, and
poetry. Included in this literature are some novel interpretations
of the *Sh'ma,* but none of his thinking is organized in a systematic

fashion. Nevertheless, by piecing together passages from different works, it is possible to see a coherent whole. One such interpretation takes into account the individual saying the *Sh'ma* before retiring to bed. Another passage addresses the *Sh'ma* as the confession of the Jewish nation. The two, however, are interrelated. Kook's philosophy is organic; what happens on one level is a reflection of all the others.

On the level of the individual, Rabbi Kook offers a particularly mystical understanding of the meaning of saying the *Sh'ma* when one goes to sleep. He begins by highlighting a few lines from the Babylonian Talmud as the basis of his interpretation. The Talmud states that saying the *Sh'ma* at night as a person goes to sleep is like going to bed with a double-edged sword.[2] Kook acknowledges that this is a strange metaphor. What are the two edges of the sword that the *Sh'ma* represents? And why should this prayer be compared to a weapon?

We must remember that going to sleep and losing consciousness was seen by ancient peoples as venturing into unknown and dangerous territory. A person's soul might go wandering during sleep, and demonic forces waited to attack the vulnerable. Saying the *Sh'ma* before sleep, therefore, was fortification against the demons of the night that could come into dreams.

Kook took the meaning of this practice one step further. He states that when people are awake, they can fight off the evil impulses in the mind. It is possible, when fully conscious, to resist temptation with the intellect. During sleep, however, the darker passions of the soul are revealed, and this leaves an impression on the body in the morning. While awake, the body and spirit are defended by the intellect, but while asleep they are open to the demons of the unconscious.

The physical saying of the *Sh'ma,* therefore, is like a sword that defends both body and spirit. Kook understood the power of the *Sh'ma* to be a spiritual defense against our own wicked impulses. The two edges of the sword, our intellectual powers while awake and the physical act of saying the *Sh'ma* before going to sleep, unite to defend our spirit. Mind and body join to protect the soul.[3]

When an individual recites the *Sh'ma,* therefore, the physical and spiritual parts of that person's being unite, like two edges of a sword. Kook's second interpretation of the *Sh'ma* offers a parallel meaning for the people Israel as a whole. In this interpretation, he cites a different passage from the Talmud, one that quotes a verse from a poem found in the book of Numbers: "They [the Israelites] crouch, they lie down like a lion, like the king of beasts, who dare rouse them?" (Numbers 24:9). In this verse from the Torah, the people Israel are compared to a mighty lion. As a nation, they are strong, and other nations fear to disturb or attack them. The Talmud says that this verse about national strength is so important that it should have been recited in conjunction with the *Sh'ma.*

Why is this verse so important, and what does this have to do with the *Sh'ma?* The Talmud does not tell us, only that the Rabbis did not want to take out only one line of a poem and that the entirety of the passage was too long and burdensome to include in the daily prayers.[4]

Kook, however, produces his own explanation as to why the idea of the Israelites lying down like lions is related to the *Sh'ma.* He says that so long as the Jewish people proclaim the unity of God, they will endure through history as God's servants. Israel's reason for being is to declare the oneness of God to all the world, and so long as they do so, they can go to sleep and rest at ease. Their mission will make them eternal.[5]

Kook thus offered similar interpretations of the *Sh'ma* for both the individual Jew and for the Jewish people as a corporate entity. For Kook, the *Sh'ma* has implications for both. Just as the individual goes to sleep fortified by saying the *Sh'ma,* so can the nation of Israel take comfort, sleeping like a lion, so long as it keeps the unity of God at the forefront of its mission. In offering this interpretation, Kook is implicitly referring to a kabbalistic notion that each individual is a microcosm of the whole. According to Jewish mysticism, the soul of every person is a universe in miniature, for the soul of an individual is a small portrait of the entirety of creation.[6] The soul of a person and the soul of the universe are linked. Similarly, each individual Jew represents the entirety of the people Israel.

Kook expressed this connection between each individual Jew as part of the Jewish people as a whole this way:

> Deep in the heart of every Jew, in its purest and holiest recesses, there blazes the fire of Israel.... This yearning for a true life, for one that is fashioned by all the commandments of the Torah and illumined by all its uplifting splendor, is the source of the courage which moves the Jew to affirm, before all the world, his loyalty to the heritage of his people, to the preservation of its identity and values, and to the upholding of its faith and vision.[7]

Each individual Jew, therefore, is called upon to take up the national mission of proclaiming the unity of God. For Kook, this must be an integral part of Zionism. The revival of the Jewish spirit depends upon each Jewish person embracing both the physical task of rebuilding the Land of Israel and the spiritual quest to fashion a nation dedicated to the Eternal. The individual pioneer is reflective of the group, and the group, united in its mission, proclaims a greater unity, that of the hope for a nation that reflects God's dominion. Such an individual is God's servant, who, like Abraham of old, will stand for God in the Promised Land.

> How this lion of a man breaks out of his confinement, how angrily he takes his staff in hand, breaks the idols and calls with a loud voice for the light, for one God, the God of the universe.[8]

Tolerance

For Kook, the *Sh'ma* is ultimately about unity: the unity of the Jewish people, the unity of the universe as an act of creation, and the unity of consciousness with God. To proclaim the *Sh'ma* means to reveal this unity. For Kook, this is the highest truth:

> The affirmation of the unity of God aspires to reveal the unity in the world, in man, among nations, and in the entire content of existence, without any dichotomy between action and theory, between reason and the imagination. Even the dichotomies experienced will be unified through a higher enlightenment, which recognizes their aspect of unity and compatibility. In the content of man's life this is the basis of holiness.... This is the most august thought among the great thoughts that man's intellectual capacity can conceive.[9]

If the Jewish people, and ultimately all the world, are all one, then this has an ethical consequence for Kook: tolerance. The conventional dichotomies that Kook struggled against in his life, such as secular versus religious or Zionist versus universalistic, all eventually led back to God. If God is one, we ought to strive for unity and harmony with each other.

Some might be threatened by being tolerant of others, as if by doing so one is admitting to the correctness of an opponent's opinion. This was especially prevalent in the Orthodox view of the secular Zionist pioneers. If one fraternized with them, is not one condoning their rejection of religion? Or perhaps one risked becoming tainted by their outlook? After all, monotheism began as an effort to reject idolatry. Perhaps intolerance has greater religious authenticity with the Jewish past.

Kook did not believe this was the case. First of all, he felt that much of Jewish tradition is founded upon legal disagreements and challenges. It is through questioning and arguing with one another that a greater truth is realized. The legal principle that "Torah scholars increase wholeness/peace [*shalom*] in the world" means that truth is a dialectical venture.[10] By voicing disagreement with each other, ideological opponents clarify the truth rather than cloud it.

But Kook also had a deeper reason to uphold the value of tolerance. For him, tolerance was a stance of faith:

> When tolerance in the realm of ideas is inspired by a heart that is pure and free of every kind of evil, it is not likely to dim the feelings of holy enthusiasm that are part of the contents of simple religious faith, the source of the happiness of all life. On the contrary, it will broaden and enhance the basis of the enthusiasm dedicated to God. Tolerance is equipped with a profound faith, reaching a point of recognizing that it is impossible for any soul to become altogether devoid of holy illumination, for the life of the living God is present in all life.[11]

By recognizing that there is a part of God in all life, even in our opponent, we are led to a sense of tolerance built upon religious faith. Even when we disagree with another deep in our soul, it is important to remember that our enemy, too, has a soul given by God.

Rabbi Kook believed that no single path could grasp all of God's truth, nor was any creation of God devoid of some spark of the divine. These intuitions gave him a basis to deal with all sorts of people, even Jews whom he considered to be transgressors. While uncompromising in his vision of the truth, he did not let his sorrow at another's heresy turn into intolerance.[12] He felt, in fact, there was always something to learn, even from the person with whom he completely disagreed. For Kook, the true enemy is narrow-mindedness, and the ideal is freedom of thought. Freedom should be used to seek the truth and meaning in life, and within this pursuit pluralism can thrive.[13]

This kind of relativism was not a form of moral equivalence; Kook heatedly condemned that which he felt was ethically wrong. He was able, however, to seek out the good in others. His association with the secular Zionists was founded on the idea that, whether they realized it or not, they were doing God's work. Whether or not they believed in God did not change the fact that they were restoring the Jewish homeland. Kook further believed that simply by living in the Land of Israel, some of them might eventually be moved to see the power of God in their lives as they resurrected the Jewish national spirit.

> How should men of faith respond to an age of ideological ferment which affirms all of these values in the name of nationalism and denies their source, the rootedness of the national spirit, in God? To oppose Jewish nationalism, even in speech, and to denigrate its values is not permissible, for the spirit of God and the spirit of Israel are identical. What they must do is work all the harder at the task of uncovering the light and holiness implicit in our national spirit, the divine element which is its core. The secularists will thus be constrained to realize that they are immersed and rooted in the life of God and bathed in the radiant sanctity that comes from above.[14]

Kook's hope was that the State of Israel would become one where all Jews felt God's presence. He wanted it to become a Jewish homeland not just physically as a haven for refugees but also spiritually in the light of the Torah. His dream was that all Jews would be able to stand on Israel's soil and recite the *Sh'ma* together as one.

"Hearing" Kook: Pluralism and Israel Today

What would Rabbi Abraham Isaac Kook have to say about the State of Israel today? It is difficult to say. After all, opponents across Israel's ideological spectrum all claim him as their mentor. Some see his view of the relationship between the Land of Israel and the people of Israel as justification for the religious settlement of the land to bring the Messiah and to create a state informed by Torah. Others cite his tolerance of others and his view that all people are made in the divine image as a rationale for compromise with Israel's Arab neighbors.[15]

What can be said with confidence is that Rabbi Kook would have believed the State of Israel at the beginning of the twenty-first century still has a long way to go to become the country he envisioned. On the one hand, he probably would have been proud of many accomplishments: the Jewish state has served as a refuge for Jews around the world, Israelis have produced miracles of science and agriculture, and there exists a functioning democracy in the Middle East attempting to engender tolerance among its citizens. On the other hand, he most likely would have been disappointed in the secular nature of the state and that the Zionist pioneers' descendants did not become religious Jews simply by being on the ancestral soil. He also would have been disappointed by the Orthodox community's inability to deal with secularism and their complete intolerance of others outside their circle. While Israel's population is a diverse one, the chief rabbinate has rejected pluralism ideologically. This has caused great tension within Israel.

If one meaning of the *Sh'ma* is unity, then this necessarily dictates the inclusion of others. One path the Jewish people might take is to seek unity with each other through greater devotion to pluralism. Some, like Kook, believed that diversity within unity enhances life, and each person is ultimately a creation of the one God. While there are great differences among Jewish people, there is also far more in common. The Jewish people can still be a "light to the nations" (Isaiah 49:6) by demonstrating wholeness and harmony.

Hear O Israel,

YHVH is our God nearby and

YHVH is the one above!

שמע ישראל

יי אלהינו

יי אחד

One Moral Standard

Leo Baeck

A Sacred Story

The teacher cleared his throat. He appeared dapper, even under the worst of circumstances. His beard and glasses gave his face a look of intelligence that no hunger or suffering could take away. His students, some sitting on the floor, others leaning out of their wooden barracks, strained to hear to his voice.[1] His bow tie and jacket came from another world, and his words spoke of ideas that belonged to another realm, a different time and place.

The man was Rabbi Leo Baeck (1873–1956), one of the last great leaders of German Jewry during the twentieth century. In the year 1933, he had been elected to the head of the Reichsvertretung, the representative body of German Jews, yet in that same year Baeck saw the rise of Adolf Hitler and knew what it would mean for the Jewish people. He declared that "the end of German Judaism has arrived."[2]

As Jews were sent to concentration camps to be murdered, Baeck, because of his great status in the community, was given many chances to leave Europe. Each time he refused. Baeck claimed as late as 1943, after the extermination had begun, that he would stay in Germany down to the last minyan of Jews. "I will go when I am the last Jew alive in Germany," he said.[3]

Baeck was deported to Theresienstadt. Theresienstadt, though horrible, was considered a "model" camp, to be visited by outside dignitaries. This status saved Baeck's life. Because he was seventy years old and considered a "prominent" person—that is, he held special value to the Nazis—he did not have to do physical labor. Nevertheless, with inadequate food and bunks built up to four or five decks and so crowded that people did not have room to stretch out, disease and death were everyday occurrences. The hunger, the dirt, the insects, and the rats, not to mention the Nazis themselves, killed people every day.

But Baeck saw another danger. People could easily lose their sense of self and their identity in the mass of emaciated humanity. "It was like a symbol that each received his transport number. That was now his characteristic feature, was the first and most important sign of his existence. It officially ousted his name and threatened inwardly to oust his self."[4]

While in the camp, Baeck maintained a sense of dignity about him. Even with starvation and dehumanization, he remained unbroken. Baeck did his duty as a rabbi and visited the sick and the elderly. He was allowed to keep his clothes, and so he wore a jacket and tie. He reminded people that there was a life before the concentration camp. One person remarked, "Leo Baeck was untouched by Theresienstadt. He never really was there."[5]

Baeck, however, deeply felt the suffering of those around him. He also felt the cold and occasionally fell ill. Nevertheless, he said prayers for the dead and was available to sit and listen. Most of all, Baeck taught.

It was at six o'clock when people would gather in the camp. People gathered around him, wherever they could find a spot, and they listened. He stood before them like a prophet, and it was as if he were in a university lecture hall, not a concentration camp. His first lecture series was on Plato, which he remembered by heart from the Greek. Then came a series on Kant, and then Spinoza, and finally Maimonides. The Nazis allowed these lectures because they did not understand them. Jews, Catholics, and Protestants attended, no matter how cold and hungry they were. The lectures ended by eight o'clock, when the people had to report to their barracks. For those two hours, they felt human again.

Baeck's final topic was the history of "this people Israel." He talked of their long existence, how they always survived. He spoke of the ethics of the prophets, and God as the one Source of justice and right. And he spoke of faith, that "beyond history and revealing itself within it, there dwells the great patience. World history has become patient justice."[6] People understood what he meant and drew strength from his words.

Baeck survived the camp, and he made a new home in London. He took the notes that he wrote while in Theresienstadt from his lectures and put them together for the first half of what would be his most important book, *This People Israel.*

Among the words from his time in the camp were these:

> "Hear O Israel, [YHVH] is our God, [YHVH] is one. You shall love YHVH with all your heart, with all your soul, with all your might" (Deuteronomy 6:4–5). In these words this people speaks to itself; these words are its prayer and confession. To possess God as the One, to remain united with him forever and everywhere, to accept God's covenant as one's own—here is the belief in God, the love of God.[7]

Remaining "united" with God "forever and everywhere" takes on new meaning when we understand the context of that utterance. Even in the midst of unspeakable horror, Baeck and others like him were still able to feel a connection with God, even "love." They insisted upon it.

An Act of Transcendence

What did it mean when Jews in concentration camps continued to say the *Sh'ma?*

To affirm the oneness of God, even under these incomprehensible circumstances, was a heroic act of spiritual resistance. In order to attempt to fully grasp the significance of this, let us look from a distance at the evil that the Jewish people confronted.

The Nazis murdered six million Jews in the Holocaust, more properly called in Hebrew the "Shoah," which means "catastrophe." (The word "Holocaust" refers to a sacrificial offering that is burned up entirely.) Of these six million, one and a half million of the victims were children. Before they were murdered and thrown into mass graves or shoved into crematoriums, the Nazis set about a specific program of dehumanizing their victims. Because the Nazis believed the Jews were vermin, they wanted to prove it to themselves by starving and working Jews into being animals before extinguishing their lives. They used the most modern technology of science and engineering in order to accomplish this goal, and they had the overwhelming, enthusiastic support of the citizens of Germany and Poland. The concentration camp, therefore, became a planet of death unto itself, removed from the rest of the world, and the large majority of Jews perished. One survivor of Auschwitz refers to those who became overwhelmed as the *Muselmänner*, for which there is no adequate translation:

> They, the *Muselmänner*, the drowned, form the backbone of the camp, an anonymous mass, continually renewed and always identical, of non-men who march and labor in silence, the divine spark dead within them, already too empty to really suffer. One hesitates to call them living: one hesitates to call their death death, in the face of which they have no fear, as they are too tired to understand.[8]

Nevertheless, there are some who did not succumb, mostly because of blind luck. Of those who were fortunate enough not to be caught up in the dehumanizing trap, there were a few of exceptional constitution who still sought meaning in life. These few had faith, and some of them, we know, still felt the commanding voice of God. Leo Baeck was one of these few, and he enabled others around him to not succumb to despair.

Baeck was able to resist, but Baeck was a "prominent" prisoner in a "model" camp. Others, however, in much worse conditions, who starved in death camps, resisted as well. There were those who asked questions of Jewish law, wondering how they could obey God's will in such circumstances.[9] Such questions themselves were a category of resistance. There were others who continued to pray and keep their minds alive. And there were those who said the *Sh'ma* and affirmed the existence of God.

Leo Baeck, during the Shoah, taught that human beings were not alone. God was not only far up above them, transcendent, but also close by, in their hearts. God was both far and yet near, and they could still feel connected to God no matter what their circumstances. The secret of the *Sh'ma* was that it contained both the words "YHVH is our God," nearby and connected to us, as well as "YHVH is one," up above and beyond the reach of human limitations. Judaism understands God as both intimate and yet infinite, and the unity of these two feelings is what Jews mean when they say, "God is one." Baeck explains it poetically this way, which he describes as nothing less than the meaning of life:[10]

> There is a paradox which welds into a unity the feelings of separation and belonging, of the here and the beyond, the exalted and the intimate, the distant and the near, the mystery and the revealed, and the miracle and the law. God is the nameless, the incomprehensible and the unattainable, and yet he [God] created my life.... The Jewish religion is conscious of the unity of both of these apparent opposites ... transcendence and immanence.[11]

For Baeck, the *Sh'ma* meant that just when people could feel most abandoned and alone, they were still connected to something beyond that gave their life meaning. This was a universal connection given to all humanity but especially manifested in the Jewish people, who were the originators of monotheism. More than just a spiritual connection, Jews could still feel commanded by God to be

ethical human beings. Rather than surrender and become dehu-
manized, it was possible to feel God commanding them, ordering
them to remember their morality and reminding them that God
had not forgotten them. Baeck wrote the following words in the
concentration camp:

> Out of the concealed, the distant, the beyond, out of the
> unique, the One, out of the eternal, infinite I, the inex-
> orable *Thou shalt* reaches every man, quite intimate, quite
> clear. He now becomes Thou, named thus by the One. To
> everyone, wherever he might be, the word of the One God
> comes as a command, and simultaneously as a promise.[12]

Baeck did not merely preach these words; he lived them. By offering lectures on philosophy to the other inmates under Nazi
oppression, his life was an act of duty and transcendence. He was
able to reach up to God with his dignity and compassion, and he
was able to bring down God to those around him who had forgotten that "the One" above was also "our God" down here. Baeck
understood God to be far, yet near, and this sense of oneness gave
him faith and strength.

Was the Connection Severed?

The experience of Baeck and other faithful was not universal.
There was the large majority of victims who became *Muselmänner,*
who were overwhelmed and for whom life lost meaning. They
could not say the *Sh'ma;* they could not even enunciate its syllables.
It would be less than honest not to say that many did feel abandoned by God, that legitimately they could no longer believe.

Elie Wiesel spoke of one such moment in his life when the
Sh'ma would have been meaningless. He recorded in his biography of
his time in the concentration camp, *Night,* the execution of a little
boy by hanging. The entire camp of Auschwitz was forced to watch.

"Where is God now?"

And I heard a voice within me answer him:

"Where is He? Here He is—He is hanging here on this gallows...."[13]

Many people have asked whether or not, for some, the connection was severed between God and the Jewish people during the Shoah. One student of Leo Baeck's, Emil Fackenheim, was not sure that "the basic principle of Judaism, the intimacy of the infinite," could be maintained in such a circumstance.[14] Fackenheim, a rabbi and a Jewish philosopher, even suggests that theology after the Shoah might be obscene.

But Fackenheim believes all must admit that there were some, even in the worst circumstances, who felt commanded by God to live. Even though Jewish faith may have been shattered into fragments, there were those in the very heart of the catastrophe who still felt God commanding them to live as righteous human beings. It is on the basis of these survivors' experiences that we are enabled to have faith as well.

Fackenheim knows that the question is not, why did so many people become *Muselmänner*? The real question is, how did anyone not become one? He bases his faith on the faith of survivors who were able to affirm the existence of God even in the face of radical evil. He cites the experience of a woman named Pelagia Lewinska, who wrote:

> At the outset the living places, the ditches, the mud, the piles of excrement behind the blocks, had appalled me with their horrible filth.... And then I saw the light! I saw that it was not a question of disorder or lack of organization but that, on the contrary, a very thoroughly considered conscious idea was in the back of the camp's existence. They had condemned us to die in our own filth, to drown in mud, in our own excrement. They wished to abase us, to destroy our human dignity, to efface every vestige of humanity, to return us to the level of wild animals, to

fill us with horror and contempt toward ourselves and our fellows.

> But from the instant that I grasped the motivating principle ... it was as if I had been awakened from a dream.... I felt under orders to live.... And if I did die in Auschwitz, it would be as a human being, I would hold on to my dignity. I was not going to become the contemptible, disgusting brute my enemy wished me to be.... And a terrible struggle began which went on day and night.[15]

For Jewish thinkers like Fackenheim, the testimony of people like Lewinska enables us to say the *Sh'ma* today. While our voices may shake at the memory of the recent past, we can still say the words and believe them.

Perhaps one of the most remarkable accounts of spiritual connectedness to the one God comes from the memory of a Jewish psychologist named Viktor Frankl. Viktor Frankl was deported to Auschwitz, where he was convinced he was doomed. He was not even sure anyone was going to miss him, as he had no children, and the one thing he felt was his contribution to humanity was the manuscript of a book that he had written but not yet published, a sheaf of papers that he kept in his coat. Upon arriving in Auschwitz, however, he was stripped of his clothes, and so he lost even this last thing of value. He was on the brink of despair, of losing all hope that life might have some meaning, when he experienced a call to live:

> Let me recall that which was perhaps the deepest experience I had in the concentration camp.... It did not seem possible, let alone probable, that the manuscript of my first book, which I had hidden in my coat when I had arrived at Auschwitz, would ever be rescued. Thus, I had to undergo and to overcome the loss of my mental child. And now it seemed as if nothing and no one would survive me; neither a physical nor a mental child of my own! So I found myself

confronted with the question whether under such circumstances my life was ultimately void of any meaning.

Not yet did I notice that an answer to this question with which I was wrestling so passionately was already in store for me, and that soon thereafter this answer would be given me. This was the case when I had to surrender my clothes and in turn inherited the worn-out rags of an inmate who had already been sent to the gas chamber immediately after his arrival at the Auschwitz railway station. Instead of the many pages of my manuscript, I found in the pocket of the newly acquired coat one single page torn out of a Hebrew prayer book, containing the most important Hebrew prayer, *Sh'ma Yisrael*. How should I have interpreted such a "coincidence" other than as a challenge to *live* my thoughts instead of merely putting them on paper?[16]

Viktor Frankl found the *Sh'ma* in the midst of human evil, and it gave him new life and purpose. Frankl would live to be not only a great psychologist but a great humanitarian, helping people find meaning in their lives. For Frankl as well as for others, the connection to the oneness of God was not severed. If he could say this prayer and mean it under those circumstances, so can we in our present day.

One Humanity and One Moral Standard

Perhaps the key to saying the *Sh'ma* after the Shoah is to look beyond the Talmudic principle that "each Jew is responsible for the other."[17] As our world has grown closer and more interconnected, we realize that all human beings, regardless of background, are responsible for each other. Whether we like it or not, we are dependent upon strong relationships with allies, on the willingness to act by all good people. We are one human family, and when one nation acts out against its citizens, we are watching the death of our brothers and sisters, no matter what their race or religion. Belief in one God means belief in one moral standard for one human family.

Baeck anticipated this belief as the necessary correlation of the Jewish belief in one God when he said, "Monotheism means, in its very essence, the oneness of all morality."[18] We do not live just to survive, nor do we live in isolation from other human beings. It is through our morality that we come to realize the one God. The Jewish people long ago gave the world the belief in one God. It is time to also give the world belief in one humanity. The Jewish people are the particular vehicle of God to teach the world the lessons of ethical monotheism.

> [The people Israel's] predominant aspect from the very beginning was its ethical character, the importance it attached to the moral law. Ethics constitutes its essence. Monotheism is the result of a realization of the absolute character of the moral law; moral consciousness teaches about God....
>
> Only in Israel did an ethical monotheism exist, and wherever else it is found later, it has been derived directly or indirectly from Israel. The nature of this religion was conditioned by the existence of the people Israel, and so it became one of the nations that has a mission to fulfill. That is what is meant by the *election* of Israel.[19]

One of the reasons the Shoah happened is because good people turned aside and let it happen. Whether it was next-door neighbors or neighboring nations around the globe, most were silent bystanders. It is one of the tragic ironies of history that the very people who brought to the world the message of one God and universal ethics for all human beings, that the "one God" is "our God" as well as yours, were allowed to be victims of prejudice and hate.

The Jewish task in history, therefore, is to continue to work for what the *Sh'ma* proclaims. It is the challenge that Jews, without giving up their particularity, should look out for all human beings, to stand up for the right to be different, to demand tolerance for all members of the human family under the sovereignty of one God. Baeck himself wrote, "It may well be its historic task to offer this image of the dissenter, who dissents for humanity's sake."[20]

"Hearing" the *Sh'ma* after a Century of Genocide

Rather than be an example that has shocked the world into ethical awareness, the Shoah has unfortunately mainly served as a precedent. While many have had their moral awareness raised by education about the Shoah, the conduct of the world's governments remains largely unaffected. The genocides of Rwanda, Bosnia, and Darfur serve as recent examples, and the nations have been consistent in their policies of nonintervention. No nation wants to intervene on behalf of another if it is not perceived to be part of that nation's self-interest.

The declaration of the *Sh'ma* will never be the same after the twentieth century. To declare that "YHVH is one" demands that we also seek unity with others despite ethnic or religious background. The oneness of God in the *Sh'ma* is partly our aspiration for oneness as a human race. "Hearing" the *Sh'ma* today, after a century of genocide, means also to hear another commandment: "You shall not stand idly by while your neighbor bleeds" (Leviticus 19:16).

In the Torah the people Israel were on a quest to reach the Promised Land. Today, our task is to realize a Promised World.

שמע ישראל

Hear O Israel,

יי אלהינו

YHVH is the living God,

יי אחד

YHVH is the one in search of us!

A Prophecy—"One World or No World"

Abraham Joshua Heschel

A Sacred Story

On March 21, 1965, religious leaders gathered with Dr. Martin Luther King, Jr., in Selma, Alabama, to protest the inability of African Americans to register to vote in the United States. Two weeks before, a similar march had taken place from the Brown Chapel toward U.S. Highway 80, only to be stopped by bigoted police officers armed with bullwhips, rubber hoses strung through with barbed wire, and tear gas. That day had ended in violence. Fifty African Americans had been hospitalized. This next gathering with Dr. King was larger and had more publicity. Three thousand black and white men and women gathered to make a statement for human rights and dignity.[1] In the front row, arms linked in a chain with Dr. King, was Rabbi Abraham Joshua Heschel.

Heschel's flowing white hair and beard made him stand out from all the rest. Around his neck and around the necks of several others was a wreath of flowers. He was marching representing Judaism's sense of ethics. On a more spiritual level, Heschel marched because he knew it was what God expected of him. He was also marching because Dr. King was his friend and had personally invited him to walk alongside him. In fact, it was at the earlier march on Washington that King had used Heschel's translation of Amos 5:24 (as opposed to the more familiar King James version) in his famous "I Have a Dream" speech: "Let justice roll down like waters, and righteousness like a mighty stream."[2] Their affection and respect were real; both referred to each other not only privately as friends but publicly as prophets.[3]

Reflecting upon it afterwards, Heschel knew that the march on Selma was of great religious significance to him. He later remarked that during the march, he felt "as though my legs were praying."[4] He wrote to King:

> The day we marched together out of Selma was a day of sanctification. That day I hope will never be past to me— that day will continue to be this day. A great Hasidic sage compares the service of God to a battle being waged in war. An army consists of infantry, artillery, and cavalry. In critical moments cavalry and artillery may step aside from the battle-front. Infantry, however, carries the brunt. I am glad to belong to infantry! May I add that I have rarely in my life been privileged to hear a sermon as glorious as the one you delivered at the service in Selma prior to the march.[5]

Rabbi Heschel marched on that day, and a black and white photograph taken of him in the front line has become a symbol for Jewish concern in human rights. In a diary entry, Heschel bemoaned the fact that not enough Jewish institutions had pledged their support. More disturbing to him was that there were many Jews involved in this nonviolent movement for civil rights, but most did not know that their Judaism compelled such action. The Hebrew prophets of the Bible had commanded in God's name to speak out in defense of others. "The vast majority of Jews participating actively in it are totally unaware of what the movement means in terms of prophetic traditions."[6]

For Heschel, to stand and be concerned for others was a Jewish duty. It is the call of the one God to the righteous, a voice that started sounding when the Israelites discovered freedom from slavery in Egypt, a voice that can still be heard today:

> The voice of God is not always inaudible.... "Every day a
> voice goes out of Mount Horeb which the righteous men
> perceive. This is meant by *Hear O Israel*: Israel, thou, hear
> the voice that proclaims all the time, at every moment:
> [YHVH] is our God, [YHVH] is One."[7]

The voice of the *Sh'ma* is the voice of the living God to good men
and women concerned with the fate of humanity. Heschel's understanding of the *Sh'ma* is directly linked to his belief in the necessity
of righteous actions. The righteous hear the *Sh'ma* and see the dire
necessity for unity. Echoing Leo Baeck and others like him, he
claimed:

> In our own age we have been forced into the realization
> that, in terms of human relations, there will be either one
> world or no world. But political and moral unity presup-
> poses unity as a source; the brotherhood of men would be
> an empty dream without the fatherhood of God.[8]

Heschel's life was an illustration of this belief. It was the *Sh'ma* in
action. In order to understand Heschel's writing, we have to
understand who he was as a rabbi, a Jew, and a human being.

Scholar and Activist

Rabbi Abraham Joshua Heschel (1907–1972) was born in Warsaw,
Poland, to a prestigious family of Hasidic Jews. While he was raised
in a traditional Jewish home, he attended the University of Berlin
and the Reform rabbinical seminary in that same city. He earned
his PhD in 1933, studying the consciousness of the Hebrew
prophets.

    With the rise of Nazism, Hebrew Union College of Cincinnati
invited him to come teach in 1940 in the United States, along with
several other scholars. This was not simply an invitation to come
lecture. It was really an effort to save his life, and Heschel left
Europe. He soon thereafter became part of the faculty at the

Jewish Theological Seminary of America in New York, the
Conservative Movement's rabbinical school. Heschel would spend
the next decades writing what would become some of the most
widely read spiritual writing of the twentieth century, including his
book *The Sabbath* and a reworking of his doctoral dissertation, *The
Prophets.*

In addition to writing many thoughtful and inspiring works in
poetic English on Jewish thought, Heschel also lived the life of a
social activist. Heschel was not only involved in the civil rights
movement, but he also actively protested the Vietnam War. In reference to that conflict, Heschel wrote, "In a free society, some are
guilty and all are responsible."[9] He also met with Pope Paul VI in
pursuit of strengthening Jewish-Christian relations by the Vatican
Council II. That council famously reversed Church doctrine by
denying Jewish guilt with regard to the crucifixion.[10]

In light of his writings and achievements for human rights
and reconciliation, Heschel has been described as not only a great
man of words but also a great man of action.[11]

Divine Concern

Heschel considered the *Sh'ma* as a confession of God's oneness to
be of ultimate importance to the Jewish people and the world. He
states, "Nothing in Jewish life is more hallowed than the *Sh'ma*."[12]

In one of Heschel's central works, *Man Is Not Alone*, he reviews
some of the meanings of the *Sh'ma* that have already been offered.
He believes that "one" has many definitions, all of which comple-
ment each other. With Moses Maimonides, he agrees that "God is
one" means more than "one among many." God cannot be indi-
cated by a number. Further, he claims that "one" can mean
"unique" and "incomparable." Heschel also denies the existence of
other powers by understanding "one" to also mean "only."[13] He
summarizes these ideas of transcendence when he says, "Eternity is
another word for unity."[14] In other words, Heschel stands upon the
foundation of the thinkers who came before him.

We ask about God. But what is the minimum of meaning that the word God holds for us? It is first the idea of *ultimacy*. God is a Being beyond which no other exists or is possible. It means further One, unique, eternal. However, all these adjectives are auxiliary to the noun to which they are attached. In themselves they do not express the essence. We proclaim, God is One; it would be intellectual idolatry to say, the One is God.[15]

Heschel, however, comes from a Hasidic background that was immersed in mysticism. In addition to the rational philosophers who preceded him, Heschel also incorporates kabbalistic thought into his understanding of God's oneness. Heschel does so when he assigns the definition of "the same" to God's oneness. By "the same" he means that concepts that are paradoxical to us are the same in reference to God. Mercy is law, and the law is mercy. The Creator is the Redeemer. God's justice and God's love, though apparently contradictory, are the same. Heschel thus holds with the mysticism of the unity of opposites.[16] Here, Isaac Luria and Abraham Isaac Kook's philosophies find expression.

Heschel adds, however, one more dimension to the idea of God's oneness. "The unity of God is a concern for the unity of the world."[17] For Heschel, an implicit idea in God's oneness is that God is concerned. The corollary of God's unity is that God cares.

Heschel challenges all those who lived before him by insisting that the one God is a living God, not a transcendent concept but a vibrant Being. The previous claims of God being incomparable, wholly unique, and infinite are essentially thoughts. Heschel does not have faith in ideas existing on their own. Instead, Heschel believes in a Supreme Being.

Our goal is to ascertain the existence of a Being to whom we may confess our sins, of a God who loves, of a God who is not above concern with our inquiry and search for Him; a father, not an absolute.... [God] is not inferior to us in the order of being. A being that lacks the attributes of

personal existence is not our problem. This, then, is the
minimum of meaning which the word God holds for us:
God is alive.[18]

Heschel's challenge to those thinkers who came before him is to
reclaim the emotional aspects of what we normally understand as
the divine. In the twelfth century, Maimonides sought to rid the
unity of God of anthropomorphisms, of any kind of human characteristics whatsoever. All such descriptions of God being "angry,"
"compassionate," or "forgiving" were to be understood purely as
symbols, whereas more rational and intellectual attributes were
higher on the scale of human perfection and closer to the divine.
If, however, the rationalists were to turn their high-powered lens of
analysis upon themselves, they would have to admit a bias. Is not
the intellect just as human as the emotions? Why ascribe rational
concepts to the Divine and leave behind only the emotions? Is this
not, in fact, subjectively limiting the possibilities of what God
might be?

Put more succinctly, why is it not possible for God to feel?
Words like unique, infinite, and even names like Creator allude to
God as an idea, power, or process. But if God "is not inferior to us
in the order of being," then the emotional components of life, and
not just the intellectual, are also a part of God's unity. The entirety
of our being points to the transcendent. Heschel's understanding
of God's oneness is more prayerful than philosophical:

> To the philosopher God is an *object,* to men at prayer He is
> the *subject.* Their aim is not to possess Him as a concept of
> knowledge, to be informed about Him, as if He were a fact
> among facts. What they crave for is to be wholly possessed
> by Him, to be an object of His knowledge and to sense it.
> The task is not to know the unknown but to be penetrated
> with it; *not to know* but *to be known* to Him, to expose our-
> selves to Him rather than Him to us; not to judge and to
> assert but to listen and to be judged by Him.[19]

Heschel attempted in his life's work to call attention to what he called the divine pathos, that is, the feeling side of God, most evident in prayer. Prayer is full of emotion, and the Jewish prayer book understands revelation to be an expression of the highest emotion, the feeling of love. The possibility of love and other emotions being a part of the Eternal does not mean, however, that God is a capricious being, ruling the universe swayed by a divine mood. Instead, the divine pathos comes from moral judgment.

> The divine pathos, whether mercy or anger, was never thought of as an impulsive act, arising automatically within the divine Being as the reaction to man's behavior and as something due to peculiarity of temperament or propensity. It is neither irrational nor irresistible. Pathos results from a decision, from an act of will. It comes about in the light of moral judgment rather than the darkness of passion.[20]

For Heschel, God's existence and unity mean that God transcends all parts of the human experience: intellectual, ethical, and emotional together. If we are alive, then at minimum God is also alive in some fashion. The living God confronts us and has concern for us. Similarly, Heschel feels, we ought to encounter the world and each other. As one Rabbinic phrase has it, "Know before whom you stand."[21]

> *Know before Whom you stand* ... [The phrase says "whom" and not "what."] To have said *what* would have contradicted the spirit of Jewish prayer.... If God is a *what,* a power, a sum total of values, how can we pray to it? An "I" does not pray to an "it." Unless, therefore, God is at least as real as my own self; unless I am sure that God has at least as much life as I do, how can I pray?[22]

We are then called upon to encounter the world and be concerned for each other. This, for Heschel, is the meaning of human existence. "God in the universe is a spirit of concern for life.... *To be* is *to stand for,* to stand for a divine concern."[23]

Wonder and Search

How does Heschel, or anyone for that matter, know of God's concern? How can we be certain that we matter to the living God? Heschel asks that we look at our own personal experience as well as the testimonies left for us by tradition.

Heschel's method of writing is deliberately poetic. In his style, he tries to invoke in the reader the feeling of being in a religious situation, the kind of rare moment that many experience only a few times in their lives, such as standing before great landscapes or witnessing childbirth. By remembering our own personal moments of inspiration, we can identify with what it means to be a witness to the divine. In short, Heschel has given up trying to prove God's existence through rational demonstration or even consistent argument.[24] Instead, through poetic devices, he tries to inspire the reader to identify with what it means to stand before God. He says, "There are no proofs for the existence of the God of Abraham. There are only witnesses."[25]

Heschel believes that there exist subjective experiences that we all share, and one of them is the feeling of grandeur, which fills all of us with awe.[26] There are moments in our lives that fill us with wonder and make us ask ultimate questions about the meaning of existence or the origin of the universe. Religion is an attempt to address those ultimate questions. Without these questions and a response to them, life seems less valuable.[27] To encounter the ineffable, for Heschel, is the beginning of wisdom.[28]

> The stirring in our hearts when watching the star-studded sky is something no language can declare. What smites us with unquenchable amazement is not that which we grasp and are able to convey but that which lies within our reach but beyond our grasp; not the quantitative aspect of nature but something qualitative; not what is beyond our range in time and space but the true meaning, source, and end of being, in other words, the ineffable.[29]

Experiencing "the ineffable" is what grounds Heschel's faith. What Jewish tradition tries to do is transmit "a legacy of wonder" from generation to generation so that each person will live in a state of "radical amazement."[30] In such a state, people feel certain that there lives a God. The problem, Heschel claims, is not one of skepticism or that human beings cannot find God in their lives. The real problem is that people take their lives for granted and are insensitive to the ever-present address of the divine. It is not we who pursue God by cataloguing our ideas and walling off our minds; it is God who searches for us:

> This is the mysterious paradox of Biblical faith: *God is pursuing man....* For God is not always silent, and man is not always blind.... Some of us have at least once experienced the momentous realness of God.[31]

Through these moments of inspiration, we either receive the voice of the divine or choose not to listen. Perhaps this is Heschel's understanding of what it means to "hear" the *Sh'ma*. It means to pay attention to the ineffable and try to find meaning beyond the mystery of existence.

Such a pursuit, Heschel teaches, is an act of divine concern. God is pursuing us because the emotional life of God is intimately caught up in the deeds of humankind. How we treat each other, whether or not we support the poor and the vulnerable, and the integrity of justice in society, as evidenced by biblical commandments and the words of the prophets, are of perpetual concern to God.

Prophetic Living

Heschel asks us to found our faith not only on our own personal moments of inspiration but also on the heritage that has been passed down to us. Past generations have lived and recorded spiritual literature to bear witness to their astonishment at the divine and the commands that God demanded of them. Our Scripture is testimony to the poetic utterances of people's experience with God.

For Heschel, the prophets are exemplars of hearing the ineffable and feeling God's presence. They felt that God pursued them and compelled them to speak out to their community. They were gripped by the emotional life of God, the divine pathos, and could not help but attempt to communicate in inadequate poetry the feelings of the living God. The biblical prophet was not a predictor of the future, as is commonly misunderstood. A prophet was a spokesperson for God, a messenger who was on a mission.

> The prophet hears God's voice and feels His heart. He tries
> to impart the pathos of the message together with its logos.
> As an imparter his soul overflows, speaking as he does out
> of the fullness of his sympathy.[32]

The prophets speak of the feelings of God. It is not just the words, but the tone with which they are said that is a part of the message. God speaks, but not through an impersonal memo. God speaks to the heart, and God's words include love, anger, disappointment, and compassion.[33]

Again, the problem is not that people are unable to relate to the prophet's message. The problem is that often people do not want to hear what the prophet is saying. Figures like Isaiah, Jeremiah, and Amos preached loudly, trying to prick their nations' conscience, but it was too difficult for some to listen to the truth. God continues to pursue the people of the world, but the people do not want to hear. Just as they shut their eyes to the needy of the world, so do they shut their ears to the voice of God. The prophet attempts to arouse the people from their self-imposed obliviousness.

> The conscience builds its confines, is subject to fatigue,
> longs for comfort, lulling, soothing. Yet those who are hurt,
> and He Who inhabits eternity, neither slumber nor sleep....
> The prophet's ear perceives the silent sigh.... The prophet
> is human, yet he employs notes one octave too high for our
> ears. He experiences moments that defy our understand-
> ing. He is neither a "singing saint" nor "a moralizing poet,"

but rather an assaulter of the mind. Often his words begin
to burn where conscience ends.[34]

It is easier, sometimes, not to listen. The command of the *Sh'ma* is
to overcome our laziness and inconveniently hear the voice of God
and the demand for unity.

With this background of Heschel's understanding of the ineffable and the legacy of the prophets, we can now better understand why he felt the voice behind the *Sh'ma* was intimately linked
to his work for civil rights. It is not only the words of the *Sh'ma* that
command unity but also the tone behind them. For Heschel, the
Sh'ma is not said neutrally but is pronounced with pathos. Heschel
personally felt that the words called to him and compelled him to
act on behalf of others.

The partnership of Rabbi Heschel and Dr. King takes on
more significance in this context. When he marched in Selma,
Heschel felt that he was acting upon a legacy dating back to the
time of the prophets of the Bible. When he referred to King as a
prophet, he had a specific model in mind, the image of a man in
sympathy with God who was voicing divine moral outrage. He saw
King as a modern-day Moses for African Americans who came to
liberate not only his people but his oppressors as well. Heschel,
too, sought the redemption of all America, white and black, and
stood as a white Jewish man among white and black activists working together. Heschel pointedly said:

> The tragedy of Pharaoh was the failure to realize that the
> exodus from slavery could have spelled redemption for
> both Israel and Egypt. Would that Pharaoh and the
> Egyptians had joined the Israelites in the desert and
> together stood at the foot of Sinai![35]

Heschel's chief affinity with King was that both felt the call of
prophetic religion, to hearken to the voice of God and make social
change. The fact that King chose to employ the Exodus from Egypt
as his chief metaphor for the civil rights movement, rather than

the story of Jesus, only drew these two men closer.[36] Each of these men sought to stir up the conscience of their constituents to make the world in greater harmony with God's will.

One of the messages that we might derive from Heschel is that monotheism means not only a statement of faith but a commandment to act. The tone of the voice behind the *Sh'ma* is insistent and demanding, not soothing. For Heschel, the *Sh'ma* can be read as a call to the prophetic spirit in each of us to stand up and be counted in the cause of justice.

"Hearing" Heschel: Social Action Today

When one hears the term "spirituality" today, too often it is simply a colorful term that covers for self-absorption. The idea of contemplating the love of God in complete isolation from others, trying to hear God's voice, is not what Abraham Joshua Heschel or the prophets of Judaism had in mind. Meditation is only a prelude to action. One enters into true spirituality with an ethical stance, knowing that deeds of righteousness are a necessary consequence of religious insight. Just as we say a blessing before we fulfill a mitzvah (divine commandment), so should prayer and reflection ultimately lead us to deeds. Social action is a religious duty.

In the Torah, there are two commandments to love. One of them is found immediately after the *Sh'ma*: "You shall love YHVH with all of your heart, with all of your soul, and with all of your might" (Deuteronomy 6:5). The oneness of God is linked to the love of God.

The other place where we are commanded to love is apparently directed elsewhere. "You shall love your neighbor as yourself" (Leviticus 19:18). Some understand this to mean that we should love the other because the other is an other, that is, for who he or she is without preconceived notions.[37] Regardless of race or religion, we are to recognize the other as a living being the same way that we each have thoughts, feelings, and families. Each is made in the image of God (Genesis 1:27).

It is an important insight that these two commandments are really one, just as God is one. Perhaps this is why the statement to love the Eternal follows the *Sh'ma*. To love God we must first learn to love our neighbor, no matter how different he or she might be.

But this kind of love is not given from afar. It is not passive. To love another means to show active concern for his or her well-being, to stand up for the other's rights and defend the other's liberties. To hear the *Sh'ma* is to hear the call of the prophetic conscience in each of us, looking for us, asking, "Where are you?" (Genesis 3:9). God is searching for us to be a partner in bringing justice, peace, and harmony to the world. One God ultimately means one hope that we human beings are empowered to make real.

שמע ישראל

יי אלהינו

יי אחד

10

"Hearing" Today

Becoming the Next Sacred Story

"Hearing"

An elderly man speaking to his people of one God of the covenant before dying.

A sage standing bleeding in a gladiators' arena, willing to offer his life only for one Power.

The head of an academy fighting for his political life, proving there is one Creator.

A famous scholar writing a letter to a student, pushing the boundaries of oneness in thought.

A disciple of mystics immersing himself in freezing water, becoming one with everything.

An outcast in a trance polishing diamonds, seeing one divine plan and goal.

A rabbi dancing the hora for one people on one land.

A beloved teacher lecturing in a concentration camp, preaching one morality.

A man with a white beard marching for civil rights and one world.

Each person "heard" God's voice differently. Each thinker was a witness to a different sense of the One.

The *Sh'ma* invokes these images and more. We could very easily add to them. Think of the disputations between Jews and Christians in Spain during the Inquisition, and of those who tried to live Christian lives on the outside while they hid and said the

Sh'ma within the relative safety of their homes. Think of the shtetls of eastern Europe and the academies of learning there, and of the Jews who lived on the fringe of the Jewish world, such as the Jewish communities of Ethiopia or China.

Most notably absent from these images are women, but due to a variety of circumstances, we do not have much of the theology of Jewish women preserved for us in writing. While these voices have always existed, contributing what must have been great insight into religious life, they have been obliterated through a lack of writing. Only with new, contemporary interpretations are these voices beginning to be heard.

What is your path to the One?

The purpose of this book is not to exclude other possibilities of the many meanings of the *Sh'ma* but to begin to truly "hear" its words. It is to start to reveal the spiritual history and the lives of important people who said the *Sh'ma* and inspire anyone who might attend a Jewish worship service to say these words with more meaning. Rather than say these six words by rote, we ought to think about what these words have meant to others in the past and what they might mean to us today. The Bible claims that God wants us to say these words with belief and to try to understand what we are saying: "Thus said YHVH to the House of Israel: Seek Me, and you will live" (Amos 5:4).

In the search for understanding, each generation used the metaphors of its age to seek out a coherent set of beliefs. The momentum of ideas in each age colored their faith. Our ancestors were unafraid to grapple with discoveries and catastrophes in their search for meaning. We, too, can be so bold in a time of post-Einstein physics, theories of evolution, historical contextualization, literary criticism, and psychological insight. The latest advances in thought do not undermine our quest for the divine. They deepen it.

What can we believe? What can we legitimately pass on to the next generation? What intellectual and spiritual tools can we employ in the search for intelligibility? If we seek answers to these questions, then we become the next sacred story in the history of the *Sh'ma*.

Bearing Witness

You do not need to be a great philosopher to take the *Sh'ma* seriously. Today everyday Jewish people encounter the *Sh'ma* in a number of instances, and it has the power to be a constant reminder of what is most important in life.

One such potential encounter is when we walk into a synagogue or Jewish home that has a mezuzah, a small, decorative box or tube containing parchment, hanging on the doorpost. The book of Deuteronomy says that we should put the words of the *Sh'ma* on our doorposts and on our gates (Deuteronomy 6:9) as a reminder of the one God whenever we enter or exit.[1] The mezuzah is hung on the right-hand side on the upper third of the doorpost, inclined inward.[2] It has become a symbol of solidarity among Jews all over the world, an expression of devotion to God, and a manifestation of the values that a Jewish home should contain. The *Sh'ma* thus serves as a reminder to people about the true foundation for their homes: "Unless YHVH builds the house, the builders labor in vain" (Psalm 127:1). Many people will kiss their fingers and touch the mezuzah when they cross the threshold, as an expression of love of being Jewish.

Another place we encounter the *Sh'ma* is in a more traditional setting. Deuteronomy also tells us that these words should be bound upon our arm and serve as a symbol upon our forehead (Deuteronomy 6:8). For centuries, Jews have wrapped tefillin, small leather boxes with leather straps containing the words of the *Sh'ma*, when they have engaged in prayer or meditation.[3] In wrapping tefillin, the worshiper accepts the sovereignty of the one God as binding. The box that is wrapped around the biceps muscle of our arm reminds us of the duty to serve God with all of our power, yet the box turns inward toward the heart, reminding us to do everything with compassion and feeling. The box on the forehead rests above our brain, telling us that our mind and all of our senses should contemplate the service of the Eternal.[4]

The most obvious place we find the *Sh'ma* is in the prayer book, or siddur. We say the *Sh'ma* in the morning and evening services, heeding the injunction to say these words when we lie down and when we rise up (Deuteronomy 6:7). They are part of the daily prayers of the Jewish people. We also proclaim the *Sh'ma* an additional time when we take out the Torah from the ark, declaring that the Torah is a gift from the one God to us.

In the prayer service, many people will close their eyes to concentrate on the words' meanings. Some will take their right hand and cover their eyes for emphasis. Depending upon the tradition of the congregation, it may be said either sitting or standing. Ultimately this is a matter of custom. A Talmudic expression affirms the plurality of Jewish practice: "Both these and these are the ways of the living God."[5]

How the prayer book presents the *Sh'ma* on the printed page reveals an essential part of its meaning for today. In almost all Hebrew prayer books, as well as in the Torah scroll itself, two letters within the *Sh'ma* are printed larger than the others. The last letter of the word *sh'ma* (hear) is the Hebrew letter *ayin,* and the last letter of the word *echad* (one) is the Hebrew letter *dalet.* These letters are not only larger, but they are also usually printed with a bolder, thicker character to make them stand out. The *ayin* and the *dalet* together form a word themselves, *eid,* which means "witness."[6]

When looking at the printing of the *Sh'ma* on the page, we are supposed to remember that we are witnesses. We testify like a witness to the belief in one God, the Jewish gift of monotheism. It can also be said that we bear witness to the past generations of the Jewish people who have uttered the *Sh'ma* and the trials that they endured.

A Suggested Meditation

The *Sh'ma* makes for a powerful phrase for meditation, and it seems to have been designed for such because of its brevity and multifaceted nature. Like all spiritual tools, saying the *Sh'ma* meditatively takes time and commitment. Saying the *Sh'ma* on a regular basis can profoundly change our lives by sensitizing us to the divine and helping us define what God means to us individually. It only takes a minute to say, but it has to be said regularly without fail to work. Spirituality is not difficult because it is complicated. It is difficult because true spirituality requires discipline. The challenge of every spiritual tool, such as saying the *Sh'ma* or lighting Shabbat candles, and so on, is that it takes regular practice. The Sages prescribed saying the *Sh'ma* twice a day, morning and evening, but this may be too much for some people. A person might try to say it once a week on the Sabbath regularly, and this can be enough to give someone a new perspective on his or her life.

The Rabbis of the Talmud were very flexible on the rules of how to say the *Sh'ma*. The most important aspect was the person's sincerity of intention. They knew that the word "hear" meant "understand," and the most important part of the discipline was for the one praying to understand what he or she was saying. It is for this reason that they decided the *Sh'ma* could be said in any language that the worshiper understands. While it was meant to be said aloud to also literally fulfill the commandment of "hearing," if a person did not do so, the obligation was still fulfilled so long as he or she understood the words.[7] Some things, however, they forbade: a person was not to repeat the *Sh'ma* over and over or change the order of the words.[8] As this was about one God, the idea is that the person praying should say it only one time. This was not a mantra to be said again and again. In addition, changing the order of the words, as we have seen, changes the meaning. The *Sh'ma* is supposed to be about unification.

Rabbi Aryeh Kaplan, a kabbalist and teacher of meditation, suggested the following with regard to using the *Sh'ma* in prayer or contemplation. To use the *Sh'ma* as a phrase for meditation cannot be rushed. We have to slow down and quiet our minds, for delving into the *Sh'ma* takes time. He teaches:

> The technique consists in saying the words very slowly.... You can dwell on each word for as long as fifteen or twenty seconds, or with experience, even longer. During the

silences between words, let the meaning of each word penetrate your innermost being.... The *Sh'ma* consists of only
six words, which are easy to memorize. Before you can use
these words as a meditation, you must know them well and
by heart.... Strive to be perfectly still, with no body motion
whatsoever.[9]

An obvious place to make the recitation of the *Sh'ma* your own spiritual discipline is at the synagogue. The *Sh'ma* is part of the order
of the prayer service, and it is surrounded by blessings. The blessings serve as bookends around it, bringing up the themes of creation, love, and redemption. These blessings naturally help to
focus one's devotion on the meaning of the prayer.

Before Our Souls Join the One

Another natural time to say the *Sh'ma* is before going to sleep.
Putting children to bed often moves us to prayer, for we are thankful
for the awesome responsibility that it is to be a parent. At the same
time, when we put ourselves to bed, it is the end of a day that is not
to be taken for granted. One sage claimed that even if a person said
the prayer in synagogue as part of the evening prayer service, the
Sh'ma could still be said again before going to sleep.[10]

Perhaps the Sages were moved to say the *Sh'ma* because a day
had passed and the transition of one day disappearing and another
beginning was not to be overlooked. Each day is a precious gift to
be appreciated and lived to the fullest.

On the other hand, perhaps the Sages were in awe of what
happens to our bodies during sleep. In saying the *Sh'ma,* a person
affirmed faith in God before the mind disappeared into dreams.
Perhaps, like many ancient peoples, they were frightened. Many
times people had gone to sleep and did not wake up. In fact, the
Rabbis claimed that sleep was the smallest possible fraction of
death.[11] Saying the *Sh'ma,* therefore, was putting your house in

order. It was seen as an act of repentance before your spirit would go wandering, perhaps not to return.

> Rabbi Eliezer said, "Repent one day before your death."
>
> His disciples asked him, "Do people know on what day they will die?"
>
> "Then all the more reason that one should repent today," he replied, "for you may die tomorrow."[12]

In this spirit there also arose the tradition of saying the *Sh'ma* on one's deathbed. When a person is ill and not going to recover, we can say the *Sh'ma*. Even if a dying person cannot say it for him- or herself, the living can gather around the bedside and say the *Sh'ma* for their loved one. Saying the *Sh'ma* is a part of a person's last atonement.

Many if not most Jewish people do not know that there is a ritual for a dying person within Jewish tradition. They think that last rites are solely within the Christian domain. The Jewish prayers before dying, however, are like a personal Yom Kippur. People repent for their sins, ask forgiveness, and offer forgiveness for others. Then the *Sh'ma* is said. Before our souls join the One, we affirm the unity of our Creator.

In many ways, the *Sh'ma* before dying is a prayer for peace of mind. Just as the Hebrew word *echad* means "one," so can it also mean "wholeness." We seek wholeness at a moment of loss. The dying desire wholeness as their life reaches its completion, and the living want wholeness as they try to work through their grief. The *Sh'ma*, in this context, is a prayer of healing. We cry out to God to make us one and complete again the way that God is one.

Finding Personal Meaning

Most people have doubts about God and are uncertain in their faith. What we believe can change, and we never know what we will believe in the future. The words of the *Sh'ma*, however, demand that we explore what we believe. More than that, they ask us to possibly change our behavior, to let these words tangibly affect our lives. These are words that are meant to be acted upon, to be lived. It is instructive, therefore, that the *Sh'ma* calls us by the name Israel when it asks us to hear God's words.

The Hebrew word *Yisrael* was given to the people in memory of their patriarch, Jacob. Jacob, the Torah tells us, received the name Israel when he wrestled with an angel of God in the night. The angel gave him the name and its explanation, meaning, "You have striven with beings divine and human and prevailed" (Genesis 32:29). Interestingly enough, Jacob prevailed not because he defeated the angel. He did not pin the angel down or knock it unconscious. Rather, Jacob was victorious because he did not let the angel go. He clung to the angel as he struggled and did not give up.

To be Israel means to struggle with God. A person need not be certain of any one belief. Akiba's protest may be most meaningful to some, whereas Maimonides's rationalism will appeal to others. Perhaps we are moved by Leo Baeck's insistence on one moral standard for humanity, while others find another meaning somewhere else. We are all like Jacob in this way, because all of us vacillate when it comes to faith. What we believe evolves throughout our lifetime, and few of us are ever free from misgivings.[13]

Jewish tradition encourages our doubts. We are supposed to ask hard questions, for then we know we are on the path of spiritual integrity.

The *Sh'ma* asks us to engage in the pursuit of faith. In saying its words, we testify to those who came before us who also engaged in this pursuit. Just as we strive to find what these words mean to us, so do we wrestle with our own personal definition of God. The most important thing is not to give up on the struggle, to cling to our personal angel, for so long as we do not surrender, we can say the *Sh'ma* wholeheartedly.

Notes

Preface

1. As God is above gender, I have refrained from referring to God using gendered language whenever possible.
2. Suzanne Gellens, *Activities That Build the Young Child's Brain* (Sarasota, FL: Early Childhood Association of Florida, 2000), 5.
3. A valuable tool for etymology, the origin of words, is www.etymonline.com.
4. See, for example, Babylonian Talmud, *Berachot*, 2B.

Chapter 1: Fighting Idolatry

1. This retelling is based upon the opening and closing chapters of the book of Deuteronomy.
2. Michael Wyschogrod, "This One and No Other," in *Ehad: The Many Meanings of God Is One,* ed. Eugene Borowitz (Port Washington, NY: *Sh'ma*, 1988), 95–98. The biblical commentator Abraham ibn Ezra (1092–1167) favored this interpretation. See his comment to Deuteronomy 6:4.
3. A very accessible and concise history of the Jewish people is Raymond P. Scheindlin, *A Short History of the Jewish People* (Oxford: Oxford University Press, 1998). He points out some important archeological finds.
4. Wyschogrod, "This One and No Other," 97.
5. This imaginative retelling relies upon 2 Kings 22–23.
6. The classic study of the gradual development of Israelite religion is by Yehezkel Kaufmann, *The Religion of Israel* (New York: Schocken Books, 1960).

7. See Sheldon H. Blank, *Understanding the Prophets* (New York: UAHC Press, 1969).

Chapter 2: The Sages Offer Their Lives

1. Babylonian Talmud, *Menachot* 29b.
2. The imaginative retelling of the life of Rabbi Akiba ben Joseph comes from many sources, including the Babylonian Talmud, *Ketubot* 62b–63a, *Berachot* 61b, *Chagigah* 14b, *Nedarim* 40a; *Avot deRabbi Natan* 6; *Tanchuma Yitro* 15; and Lamentations Rabbah 2:2. There are many other legends about his life. See also Louis Finkelstein, *Akiba: Scholar, Saint, and Martyr* (New York: Atheneum, 1975).
3. Babylonian Talmud, *Berachot* 61b.
4. Babylonian Talmud, *Berachot* 2a.
5. The best place to read all of the instructions regarding the recitation of the *Sh'ma* is in Moses Maimonides's code of Jewish law, *Mishneh Torah*, Book of Love, chapter 1.
6. *Avot deRabbi Natan* 4.
7. There was still the temptation to join other religious faiths. Most challenging to the Rabbis were the Gnostics, who held that there were two powers in the universe, a god of good and a god of evil. Dualism was very attractive in the times of antiquity. A Rabbinic parable in Deuteronomy Rabbah 2:31 directly addresses this concern: "The Holy One of Blessing said to Israel, 'My children, note that all I created, I created in pairs. Heaven and earth are a pair; the sun and the moon are a pair; Adam and Eve are a pair; this world and the world-to-come are a pair. But My glory is one and unique in the world.'"
8. Babylonian Talmud, *Sanhedrin* 74a.
9. Babylonian Talmud, *Pesachim* 25b.
10. Babylonian Talmud, *Berachot* 61b.
11. *Pirkei Avot* 3:14.
12. *Pirkei Avot* 2:6.
13. Babylonian Talmud, *Berachot* 61b.
14. See Susan L. Einbinder's comments in *My People's Prayer Book, Vol. 1, The* Sh'ma *and Its Blessings* (Woodstock, VT: Jewish Lights Publishing, 1997), 90.
15. Rashi based his comment upon *Sifrei* on Deuteronomy 6:4.
16. Babylonian Talmud, *Pesachim* 56a.

Chapter 3: Proving the One

1. Saadia Gaon, *The Book of Beliefs and Opinions*, trans. Samuel Rosenblatt (New Haven: Yale University Press, 1948), 7, 94.
2. The creative retelling of parts of Saadia's life comes from Robert Brody, *The Geonim of Babylonia and the Shaping of Medieval Jewish Culture* (New Haven: Yale University Press, 1998); Colette Sirat, *A History of Jewish Philosophy in the Middle Ages* (Cambridge: Cambridge University Press, 1985); and Samuel Rosenblatt's introduction in Saadia, *The Book of Beliefs and Opinions*, xxiii–xxxii.
3. Numbers Rabbah 9:48 and many other places. The expression in Rabbinic rhetoric indicates giving an undeserving person a flip answer, followed by giving worthy students a more thoughtful answer.
4. Saadia, *Beliefs and Opinions*, 16–19.
5. The proofs as presented here are simplifications for the uninitiated reader and risk being oversimplified. Saadia Gaon presents each of his four proofs with a certain method: a logical exposition, some refutations of expected challenges, and finally citations from Scripture for support.
6. *Midrash Temura*, 3. See Hayim Nahman Bialik and Yehoshua Hana Ravnitzky, *The Book of Legends: Sefer Ha-Aggadah, Legends from the Talmud and Midrash*, trans. William G. Braude (New York: Schocken Books, 1992), 6–7:6.
7. Bachya ben Joseph ibn Paquda, *Duties of the Heart*, trans. Moses Hyamson (Israel: Boys Town Jerusalem Publishers, 1962), 55.
8. Ibid., 79.

Chapter 4: Nothing Like God

1. A translation of Moses Maimonides's famous letter describing his daily routine can be found in Jacob S. Minkin, *The World of Moses Maimonides* (New York: Thomas Yoseloff, 1957), 154–55.
2. Interestingly, Moses Maimonides does not use the *Sh'ma* in his demonstrations of God's unity even though he codifies its centrality in his code of Jewish law, the *Mishneh Torah*.
3. Moses Maimonides, *The Guide for the Perplexed*, trans. Shlomo Pines (Chicago: University of Chicago Press, 1963), 1:57, 133.
4. Ibid., 4.
5. Ibid., 1:10, 35–37.
6. Ibid., 1:9, 34–35.
7. Ibid., 1:50, 111.
8. Ibid., 1:50, 111–12.

9. Moses Maimonides, *Mishneh Torah,* Laws on the Fundamentals of Torah 1:7.

10. The idea of negative theology, that is, not saying what God is but instead saying what God is not, is a centerpiece of Maimonides's thinking. An excellent introduction to Maimonides's philosophy is by Kenneth Seeskin, *Maimonides: A Guide for Today's Perplexed* (West Orange: Behrman House, 1991).

11. Maimonides suggests that the best possible praise of God is silence, quoting this line from the Psalms. Maimonides, *Guide* 1:59, 139.

12. Maimonides, *Mishneh Torah,* Laws of Repentance 5:1.

13. *Pirkei Avot* 3:14.

14. Babylonian Talmud, *Sanhedrin* 37a.

Chapter 5: Communing with the One

1. While later generations would refer to him as the Holy Rabbi Isaac, his contemporaries referred to him as Ashkenazi. See Gershom Scholem, *Kabbalah* (Jerusalem: Keter Publishing House, 1974), 420.

2. This imaginative scene is based upon the scholarship of Lawrence Fine, *Safed Spirituality* (Mahwah: Paulist Press, 1984), and Scholem, *Kabbalah.*

3. The hymn *L'cha Dodi* is found in the Friday night Sabbath service in the Jewish prayer book. The first letters of each verse spell the name of the author of the song, Shlomo Halevi, Solomon the Levite.

4. Moses Cordovero, *Elimah Rabbati* 24d–25a, in *The Essential Kabbalah,* trans. Daniel Matt (Edison: Castle Books, 1997), 24.

5. In philosophical terms, this is called panentheism. Panentheism means that God fills nature yet transcends it. It is distinguished from pantheism, which indicates that God is identical to nature.

6. *Zohar* 2:133b–134b, adapted from Isaiah Tishby, *The Wisdom of the Zohar* (London: Littman Library of Jewish Civilization, 1949), 1023–24.

7. Daniel Matt, *Zohar: The Book of Enlightenment* (Mahwah: Paulist Press, 1983), 1:21.

8. *Zohar* 1:12a, in Daniel Matt, *The Zohar* (Stanford: Stanford University Press, 2004), 1:82–84.

9. Moses Cordovero, *Sh'iur Komah* 206b, in *The Essential Kabbalah,* 24.

10. Scholem, *Kabbalah* 167. See Matt's translation of a selection from "Luria's Sermon in Jerusalem and the Kavannah of Eating," in *The Essential Kabbalah,* 149.

11. Based upon Babylonian Talmud, *Kiddushin* 40a–40b.

Chapter 6: "Master of the Universe"

1. This completely fictional episode is based upon the historical facts of Moses Haim Luzzatto's life.

2. This summary of Luzzatto's life is based upon the biographical sketches by Joseph Dan, "Luzzatto, Moses Hayyim," *Encyclopaedia Judaica* 11 (1972): 599–604; Simon Ginzburg, *The Life and Works of Moses Hayyim Luzzatto* (Westport: Greenwood Press, 1975); and Paul Johnson, *A History of the Jews* (New York: Harper & Row Publishers, 1987), 336–38. It should be noted that Ginzburg's work conflicts with the others. Ginzburg dismisses Kabbalah as "superstition" and laments Luzzatto's involvement in it, minimizing his role as a mystic in order to emphasize Luzzatto's talents as a dramatist in Hebrew. The apologetic nature of his biography makes many of his claims suspect. I have chosen to follow Dan's interpretation of Luzzatto's life in this chapter, particularly the theory that Luzzatto understood himself to possess the reincarnated soul of Moses, to which Ginzburg only alludes.

3. Moses Haim Luzzatto, *The Way of God*, trans. Aryeh Kaplan (Jerusalem: Feldheim Publishers, 1988), 4:4:2, 265.

4. Hebrew: *hashalit.*

5. Luzzatto, *Way of God*, 4:4:1, 259. While I have tried to use the word "God" to replace "He," as God is above gender, in kabbalistic writings gender has specific theological meaning. I have refrained from adapting the translations in this case.

6. Hebrew: *hachochma haelyona.*

7. Luzzatto, *Way of God*, 4:4:5, 271.

8. Hebrew: *shoresh.* The writers of Kabbalah play with the imagination by referring to God as a Root that comes from above. One expects a plant to grow up from the ground. The kabbalists articulated a paradox of an upside-down tree to represent the *sefirot.* The dimensions of up and down are merely metaphors.

9. Luzzatto, *Way of God*, 4:4:1, 257.

10. Hebrew: *haminaheg.*

11. Luzzatto, *Way of God*, 4:4:1, 259.

12. Ibid., 4:4:1, 263.

13. Ibid.

14. Ibid., Introduction, 21.

15. Ibid., 4:4:1, 263.

16. Luzzatto, *Essay on Fundamentals*, in *Way of God*, 393.

17. Luzzatto, *Way of God*, 4:4:3, 267.

18. Ibid., 273.

19. Lincoln Barnett, *The Universe and Dr. Einstein,* foreword by Albert Einstein (New York: Bantam Books, 1957), 108.

20. Barnett, *Universe,* 111–13.

21. I thank Rabbi Gustav Buchdahl for asking this question.

Chapter 7: A Nation Reborn

1. This biographical sketch is based upon Jacob Agus, "Avraham Yitzchak haCohen Kook: A Biographical Profile," *The World of Rav Kook's Thought,* trans. Benjamin Ish Shalom and Shalom Rosenberg (United States: Avi Chai, 1991), xv–xxix, which is a summary of Agus's comprehensive biography of Kook's life, *Banner of Jerusalem* (New York: Bloch Publishing Co., 1946). See also Howard M. Sachar, *A History of Israel: From the Rise of Zionism to Our Time* (New York: Alfred A. Knopf, 1991), 192.

2. Babylonian Talmud, *Berachot* 5a.

3. Abraham Isaac Kook, *Ein Eyah* 1:14, trans. Chanan Morrison, RavKook.n3.net,
http://www.geocities.com/m_yericho/ravkook/PSALM149.htm.
Many of Kook's works are not published, but some are available in translation on the Internet.

4. Babylonian Talmud, *Berachot* 12b.

5. Kook, *Ein Eyah* 1:67, trans. Chanan Morrison, RavKook.n3.net,
http://www.geocities.com/m_yericho/ravkook/BALAK59.htm.

6. Scholem, *Kabbalah,* 152–53.

7. Abraham Isaac Kook, "The Land of Israel," in *The Zionist Idea,* trans. Arthur Hertzberg (Philadelphia: Jewish Publication Society, 1997), 421.

8. Abraham Isaac Kook, "The Significance of the Revival," in *Abraham Isaac Kook: The Lights of Penitence, Lights of Holiness, the Moral Principles, Essays, Letters, and Poems,* trans. Ben Zion Bokser (New York: Paulist Press, 1978), 283.

9. Kook, "Lights of Holiness" 2:425, in *Abraham Isaac Kook,* 225.

10. *Shulchan Aruch, Orach Chaim* 1:330, as cited in Benjamin Ish Shalom, "Tolerance and Its Theoretical Basis in the Teaching of Rav Kook," in *Rabbi Abraham Isaac Kook and Jewish Spirituality,* ed. Lawrence Kaplan and David Shatz (New York: New York University Press, 1995), 198.

11. Kook, "The Moral Principles," *Abraham Isaac Kook,* 175.

12. Ish-Shalom, *Rabbi Abraham Isaac Kook and Jewish Spirituality,* 181.

13. Ibid., 195–97.

14. Kook, "Lights for Rebirth," in *Zionist Idea*, 430.

15. Tamar Ross, "What Would Rav Kook Have to Say about the State of Israel Today?" in *Rabbi Abraham Isaac Kook and Jewish Spirituality*, 301–07.

Chapter 8: One Humanity

1. The Pulitzer Prize–winning biography of Baeck's life from which this sketch is drawn is by Leonard Baker, *Days of Sorrow and Pain: Leo Baeck and the Berlin Jews* (New York: Macmillan Publishing Co., 1978).

2. Ibid., 145.

3. Ibid., 238.

4. Ibid., 287.

5. Ibid., 287.

6. Leo Baeck, *This People Israel: The Meaning of Jewish Existence*, trans. Albert H. Friedlander (Philadelphia: Jewish Publication Society, 1965), 37.

7. Ibid., 25.

8. Primo Levi, *Survival in Auschwitz* (New York: Macmillan Publishing Company, 1959), 82.

9. See Rabbi Ephraim Oshry, *Responsa from the Holocaust* (New York: Judaica Press, 1983). Included (Responsum 25) is a question as to how slave laborers could fulfill the commandment of reciting the morning *Sh'ma*. They went to work well before sunrise and did not receive lunch until far into the afternoon. During their labor, their oppressors constantly gave them orders and did not let them rest, much less pray. The fact that they were preoccupied with this matter shows an act of transcendence in that they were worried about heeding God's will while still under the Nazis' control.

10. The meaning of life as being the unity of transcendence and immanence is described in his essay, "Mystery and Commandment," *Judaism and Christianity* (Philadelphia: Jewish Publication Society, 1958), 171–85.

11. Leo Baeck, *The Essence of Judaism* (New York: Schocken Books, 1948), 100.

12. Baeck, *This People Israel*, 14.

13. Elie Wiesel, *Night* (New York: Bantam Books, 1960), 62.

14. Emil Fackenheim, *What Is Judaism?* (New York: Macmillan Publishing Company, 1987), 284.

15. The words of Pelagia Lewinska as quoted by Emil Fackenheim, *To Mend the World* (New York: Schocken Books, 1982), 217.

16. Viktor Frankl, *Man's Search for Meaning* (New York: Pocket Books, 1959), 137–38.

17. Babylonian Talmud, *Sanhedrin* 27b.

18. Baeck, *This People Israel,* 69.

19. Baeck, *Essence of Judaism,* 59, 61.

20. Baeck, "Mystery," in *Judaism and Christianity,* 184–85.

Chapter 9: A Prophecy—"One World or No World"

1. For a description of the march on Selma, see Harvard Sitkoff, *The Struggle for Black Equality* (New York: Hill and Wang, 1981), 174–83.

2. Susannah Heschel, "Theological Affinities in the Writings of Heschel and King," in *Black Zion: African American Religious Encounters with Judaism,* ed. Yvonne Chireau and Nathaniel Deutsch (Oxford: Oxford University Press, 2000), 173.

3. Ibid., 183.

4. Ibid., 175.

5. Abraham Joshua Heschel, letter dated March 29, 1965, cited in "Theological Affinities," 175.

6. Abraham Joshua Heschel, *Moral Grandeur and Spiritual Audacity: Essays of Abraham Joshua Heschel,* ed. Susannah Heschel (New York: Farrar, Straus, and Giroux, 1996), xxxiii–xxxiv.

7. Abraham Joshua Heschel, quoting *Zohar* 1:90a, in *God in Search of Man: A Philosophy of Judaism* (New York: Noonday Press, 1955), 145–46. I have substituted YHVH for "the Lord."

8. Abraham Joshua Heschel, *Man Is Not Alone: A Philosophy of Religion* (New York: Noonday Press, 1951), 112. For the remainder of the chapter, I leave the gender specificity of Heschel's writing unmarked.

9. Heschel, cited by S. Heschel in *Moral Grandeur,* xxxiv.

10. A short, accessible biography of Abraham Joshua Heschel is by Or N. Rose, *Abraham Joshua Heschel: Man of Spirit, Man of Action* (Philadelphia: Jewish Publication Society, 2003). While it lacks footnotes, it may inspire a reader to attempt some of Heschel's more difficult works.

11. William E. Kaufman, *Contemporary Jewish Philosophies* (Detroit: Wayne State University Press, 1976), 142–74.

12. Heschel, *Man Is Not Alone,* 114.

13. Ibid., 115–18.

14. Ibid., 112.

15. Heschel, *God in Search of Man,* 125.

16. Heschel, *Man Is Not Alone,* 118–19.

17. Ibid., 123.

18. Heschel, *God in Search of Man,* 126.

19. Heschel, *Man Is Not Alone,* 128–29.

20. Abraham Joshua Heschel, *The Prophets: An Introduction* (New York: Harper & Row, 1969–71), 2:78.

21. Babylonian Talmud, *Berachot* 28b.

22. From an address delivered before the Rabbinical Assembly of America at Atlantic City, New Jersey, in 1953, as quoted in Abraham Joshua Heschel, *Between God and Man,* ed. Fritz Rothschild (New York: The Free Press, 1959), 212.

23. Heschel, *Man Is Not Alone,* 145.

24. Some have found a lack of coherence and rationality to be a great failing of Heschel's philosophy. As Heschel's writing stands, either we identify with the religious experiences he describes or we do not. If faith is not coherent and cannot be rationally shared, then what is the point of trying to explain an incommunicable experience? Heschel himself most likely did not want his philosophy to be read as a series of disjointed aphorisms, and his hope was to allude to a transubjective experience. For a critique of Heschel's writing along these lines, see Kaufman, *Contemporary Jewish Philosophies,* 169–72.

25. Heschel, *The Prophets,* 1:22.

26. Heschel, *Man Is Not Alone,* 3.

27. Heschel, *God in Search of Man,* 3.

28. Ibid., 74.

29. Heschel, *Man Is Not Alone,* 4–5.

30. Heschel, *God in Search of Man,* 43–48.

31. Ibid., 136–38.

32. Heschel, *The Prophets,* 1:26.

33. Ibid., 1:24.

34. Ibid., 1:9–10.

35. Abraham Joshua Heschel, "The White Man on Trial," *The Insecurity of Freedom* (1966), 103, cited in "Theological Affinities," 178.

36. S. Heschel, "Theological Affinities," 172–73.

37. Baeck, *Essence of Judaism,* 190–92.

Chapter 10: "Hearing" Today

1. The mezuzah traditionally contains these passages: Deuteronomy 6:4–9, 11:13–21.

2. *Shulchan Aruch Yoreh Deah* 289:1-6.

3. The tefillin contain four passages: Deuteronomy 6:4–9, 11:13–21, Exodus 13:1–10, 13:11–16.
4. *Shulchan Aruch, Orach Chaim* 25:5.
5. Babylonian Talmud, *Eruvin* 13b, *Gittin* 5b.
6. This interpretation follows the *Zohar* 2:160b. Another explanation from the Talmud and Midrash (Babylonian Talmud, *Eruvin* 13a; Leviticus Rabbah 19:2) is that the Hebrew letter *dalet* could be confused with the letter *resh*, which has a very similar shape. That word, however, spells *acher*, meaning "another" rather than "one." This would render the opposite of the intended meaning of the *Sh'ma*. Similarly, the *ayin*, a silent Hebrew letter, might be confused with an *aleph*, which is also silent. (See Babylonian Talmud, *Yevamot* 22b, 35b, and *Bava Batra* 115a, where the *aleph* and *ayin* are interchangeable.) The word *shema* with an *aleph* and vocalized differently, however, means "perhaps," as in "Perhaps, O Israel…"
7. Babylonian Talmud, *Berachot* 13a.
8. *Mishnah Berachot* 2:3, Babylonian Talmud, *Berachot* 33b.
9. Aryeh Kaplan, *Jewish Meditation: A Practical Guide* (New York: Schocken Books, 1985), 128.
10. Babylonian Talmud, *Berachot* 4b.
11. Babylonian Talmud, *Berachot* 57b: "Sleep is one-sixtieth of death." One-sixtieth was considered the smallest possible fraction of any kind of reality. Less than this fraction was negligible and not considered significant.
12. Babylonian Talmud, *Shabbat* 153a.
13. Kaplan finds another meaning in the fact that we are called Israel. For Kaplan, the struggle is to quiet our mind. We wrestle with images, noises, and distractions so that we can meditate on God's words. See Kaplan, *Jewish Meditation*, 125.

Discussion Guide

Preface

- What is the difficulty in translating the *Sh'ma?*
- What are the different possible meanings of the word "hear"?
- Why is it important to try to understand what we are saying when we recite the *Sh'ma?*

Chapter 1: Fighting Idolatry

- What was the original meaning of the *Sh'ma* as said by Moses?
- What challenges did King Josiah face that Moses did not? Why?
- How long did it take for monotheism to take hold in the Israelites' understanding of God?
- What revolutionary claims did the prophets of Israel make, especially when the surrounding empires destroyed Israelite sovereignty?
- What forms did idolatry take in the Bible? Do some still exist today?

Chapter 2: The Sages Offer Their Lives

- What kind of person was Rabbi Akiba? In the face of Roman persecution, why was Rabbi Akiba's martyrdom inevitable?
- What does "spiritual resistance" mean? What does it mean to say the *Sh'ma* as protest?

- What are some of the meanings behind the phrase "the world-to-come"?
- What did the Jews who died in the Crusades have in common with Rabbi Akiba? What was different about their circumstances?
- Do you feel an obligation to past Jewish martyrs? Why or why not?

Chapter 3: Proving the One

- What were some of the major changes in the world that had occurred by the time of Saadia Gaon?
- What kind of person was Saadia Gaon? How did this shape his writing?
- What are Saadia's four proofs for creation?
- Explain Rabbi Akiba and Bachya ibn Pakuda's proofs. How are they similar and different to Saadia's and to each other?
- How is the idea of God as Creator linked to the *Sh'ma*'s statement that God is one?

Chapter 4: Nothing Like God

- According to Maimonides, why should we be perplexed?
- What was troubling to Maimonides about anthropomorphisms in the Bible?
- What does it mean that God is "wholly unique"? How does this relate to the *Sh'ma*?
- What problems arise with language when trying to talk about God?
- According to Maimonides, what does it mean that human beings are made in the divine image?

Chapter 5: Communing with the One

- What kind of lifestyle did the mystics of Safed lead?
- What historical circumstances shaped the birth of Kabbalah?
- How did the kabbalists think about gender? How was this represented in the *Sh'ma*?
- How did the kabbalists talk about God's presence in the world?

- What was the meaning of *tikkun olam* to the kabbalists?

Chapter 6: "Master of the Universe"

- What was scandalous about Moses Haim Luzzatto's life?
- What did Luzzatto mean when he understood God to be the Ruler of the universe?
- How did Luzzatto explain the existence of chaos in the world?
- What role did the Messiah play in Luzzatto's thinking? How is this connected to saying the *Sh'ma?*
- What other people have proposed that the world runs according to a divine pattern? How are their ideas similar to or different from Luzzatto's?

Chapter 7: A Nation Reborn

- What risks did Abraham Isaac Kook take in his life? Why?
- What did the unity represented in the *Sh'ma* mean to Kook (a) for the individual, (b) for the nation of Israel, and (c) for the world?
- What ethical values are a consequence of Kook's understanding of the *Sh'ma?*
- How did Kook try to live out these values in his life?
- What do you think Kook would say about the State of Israel today? Why?

Chapter 8: One Moral Standard

- How was Leo Baeck able to say the *Sh'ma* during the Shoah?
- What paradoxical meaning did the *Sh'ma* have for Baeck?
- What are some of the Shoah's challenges to Jewish theology and the idea of God's oneness?
- How did Emil Fackenheim try to resolve some of the Shoah's theological challenges?
- What does it mean that "monotheism demands one moral standard"?

Chapter 9: A Prophecy—"One World or No World"

- How was the *Sh'ma* related in Abraham Joshua Heschel's mind to his march on Selma?
- What are the definitions of "God is one" that Heschel offers? How does divine concern contradict some of Heschel's predecessors? What did Heschel mean when he wrote, "God is alive"?
- What is "the ineffable"? Describe moments that might foster "radical amazement."
- What is "divine pathos"? How does it relate to the life of the prophet?
- According to Heschel, how is the *Sh'ma* related to social action?

Chapter 10: "Hearing" Today

- Which figures are most meaningful to you of those presented here? Why?
- Who historically has been missing from the writing of Jewish theology?
- During what ritual moments do Jews invoke the *Sh'ma*?
- How is the idea of being a witness emphasized in the appearance of the *Sh'ma* in the Torah scroll?
- How is saying the *Sh'ma* related to facing death? Does this have personal meaning for you?
- How does the wording of the *Sh'ma* permit us to "struggle with God"?

Suggestions for Further Reading

Where Do I Go from Here?

In addition to the many primary and secondary sources cited throughout this work, the following books introduce the reader to different areas of Jewish experience and thought.

Cohen, Norman J. *The Way Into Torah.* Woodstock, Vt: Jewish Lights Publishing, 2000.

Gillman, Neil. *The Way Into Encountering God in Judaism.* Woodstock, Vt: Jewish Lights Publishing, 2000.

Hoffman, Lawrence. *The Way Into Jewish Prayer.* Woodstock, Vt: Jewish Lights Publishing, 2000.

———. *My People's Prayer Book, Vol. 1: Traditional Prayers, Modern Commentaries–The* Sh'ma *and Its Blessings.* Woodstock, Vt: Jewish Lights Publishing, 1997.

Kushner, Lawrence. *The Way Into Jewish Mystical Tradition.* Woodstock, Vt: Jewish Lights Publishing, 2001.

Scheindlin, Raymond P. *A Short History of the Jewish People.* Oxford: Oxford University Press, 1997.

Sonsino, Rifat, and Daniel B. Syme. *Finding God: Selected Responses.* New York: URJ Press, 2002.

For books from different time periods on Jewish belief or by each of the thinkers presented here, I recommend:

Alter, Robert. *The Art of the Biblical Narrative.* New York: Basic Books, 1981.

Kravitz, Leonard and Kerry M. Olitzky, ed. and trans. Pirke Avot: *A Modern Commentary on Jewish Ethics.* New York: URJ Press, 1993.

Seeskin, Kenneth. *Maimonides: A Guide for Today's Perplexed.* West Orange: Behrman House, 1991.

Matt, Daniel C. *The Essential Kabbalah.* Edison: Castle Books, 1997.

Mordecai Kaplan trans. *The Path of the Upright.* Northvale: Jason Aronson Inc., 1995.

Heschel, Abraham Joshua. *The Sabbath.* New York: Farrar, Straus, and Giroux, 1995.

Baeck, Leo. "Mystery and Commandment," *Judaism and Christianity* Philadelphia: The Jewish Publication Society of America, 1958.

Ben Zion Bokser trans. *Abraham Isaac Kook: The Lights of Penitence, Lights of Holiness, the Moral Principles, Essays, Letters, and Poems.* New York: Paulist Press, 1978.

Notes

Notes

Notes

Notes

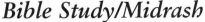

Children's Books

What You Will See Inside a Synagogue
By Rabbi Lawrence A. Hoffman and Dr. Ron Wolfson; Full-color photos by Bill Aron

A colorful, fun-to-read introduction that explains the ways and whys of Jewish worship and religious life. Full-page photos; concise but informative descriptions of the objects used, the clergy and laypeople who have specific roles, and much more. For ages 6 & up.

8½ x 10½, 32 pp, Full-color photos, Hardcover, ISBN 1-59473-012-1 **$17.99** *(A SkyLight Paths book)*

Because Nothing Looks Like God
By Lawrence and Karen Kushner

What is God like? Introduces children to the possibilities of spiritual life. Real-life examples of happiness and sadness invite us to explore, together with our children, the questions we all have about God.

11 x 8½, 32 pp, Full-color illus., Hardcover, ISBN 1-58023-092-X **$16.95** *For ages 4 & up*

Also Available: **Because Nothing Looks Like God Teacher's Guide**
8½ x 11, 22 pp, PB, ISBN 1-58023-140-3 **$6.95** *For ages 5–8*

Board Book Companions to *Because Nothing Looks Like God*
5 x 5, 24 pp, Full-color illus., SkyLight Paths Board Books *For ages 0–4*

What Does God Look Like? ISBN 1-893361-23-3 **$7.99**
How Does God Make Things Happen? ISBN 1-893361-24-1 **$7.95**
Where Is God? ISBN 1-893361-17-9 **$7.99**

The 11th Commandment: Wisdom from Our Children
By The Children of America

"If there were an Eleventh Commandment, what would it be?" Children of many religious denominations across America answer in their own drawings and words.

8 x 10, 48 pp, Full-color illus., Hardcover, ISBN 1-879045-46-X **$16.95** *For all ages*

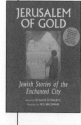

Jerusalem of Gold: Jewish Stories of the Enchanted City
Retold by Howard Schwartz. Full-color illus. by Neil Waldman.

A beautiful and engaging collection of historical and legendary stories for children. Based on Talmud, midrash, Jewish folklore, and mystical and Hasidic sources.

8 x 10, 64 pp, Full-color illus., Hardcover, ISBN 1-58023-149-7 **$18.95** *For ages 7 & up*

The Book of Miracles: A Young Person's Guide to Jewish Spiritual Awareness
By Lawrence Kushner. All-new illustrations by the author.

6 x 9, 96 pp, 2-color illus., Hardcover, ISBN 1-879045-78-8 **$16.95** *For ages 9–13*

In Our Image: God's First Creatures
By Nancy Sohn Swartz

9 x 12, 32 pp, Full-color illus., Hardcover, ISBN 1-879045-99-0 **$16.95** *For ages 4 & up*

Also Available as a Board Book: **How Did the Animals Help God?**
5 x 5, 24 pp, Board, Full-color illus., ISBN 1-59473-044-X **$7.99** *For ages 0–4 (A SkyLight Paths book)*

From SKYLIGHT PATHS PUBLISHING

Becoming Me: A Story of Creation
By Martin Boroson. Full-color illus. by Christopher Gilvan-Cartwright.

Told in the personal "voice" of the Creator, a story about creation and relationship that is about each one of us.

8 x 10, 32 pp, Full-color illus., Hardcover, ISBN 1-893361-11-X **$16.95** *For ages 4 & up*

Ten Amazing People: And How They Changed the World
By Maura D. Shaw. Foreword by Dr. Robert Coles. Full-color illus. by Stephen Marchesi.

Black Elk • Dorothy Day • Malcolm X • Mahatma Gandhi • Martin Luther King, Jr. • Mother Teresa • Janusz Korczak • Desmond Tutu • Thich Nhat Hanh • Albert Schweitzer.

8½ x 11, 48 pp, Full-color illus., Hardcover, ISBN 1-893361-47-0 **$17.99** *For ages 7 & up*

Where Does God Live? *By August Gold and Matthew J. Perlman*
Helps young readers develop a personal understanding of God.

10 x 8½, 32 pp, Full-color photo illus., Quality PB, ISBN 1-893361-39-X **$8.99** *For ages 3–6*

Children's Books
by Sandy Eisenberg Sasso

Adam & Eve's First Sunset: God's New Day

Engaging new story explores fear and hope, faith and gratitude in ways that will delight kids and adults—inspiring us to bless each of God's days and nights.

9 x 12, 32 pp, Full-color illus., Hardcover, ISBN 1-58023-177-2 **$17.95** *For ages 4 & up*

Also Available as a Board Book: **Adam and Eve's New Day**

5 x 5, 24 pp, Full-color illus., Board, ISBN 1-59473-205-1 **$7.99** *For ages 0–4 (A SkyLight Paths book)*

But God Remembered

Stories of Women from Creation to the Promised Land

Four different stories of women—Lillith, Serach, Bityah, and the Daughters of Z—teach us important values through their faith and actions.

9 x 12, 32 pp, Full-color illus., Hardcover, ISBN 1-879045-43-5 **$16.95** *For ages 8 & up*

Cain & Abel: Finding the Fruits of Peace

Shows children that we have the power to deal with anger in positive ways. Provides questions for kids and adults to explore together.

9 x 12, 32 pp, Full-color illus., Hardcover, ISBN 1-58023-123-3 **$16.95** *For ages 5 & up*

God in Between

If you wanted to find God, where would you look? This magical, mythical tale teaches that God can be found where we are: within all of us and the relationships between us.

9 x 12, 32 pp, Full-color illus., Hardcover, ISBN 1-879045-86-9 **$16.95** *For ages 4 & up*

God's Paintbrush: Special 10th Anniversary Edition

Wonderfully interactive, invites children of all faiths and backgrounds to encounter God through moments in their own lives. Provides questions adult and child can explore together.

11 x 8½, 32 pp, Full-color illus., Hardcover, ISBN 1-58023-195-0 **$17.95** *For ages 4 & up*

Also Available: **God's Paintbrush Teacher's Guide**

8½ x 11, 32 pp, PB, ISBN 1-879045-57-5 **$8.95**

God's Paintbrush Celebration Kit

A Spiritual Activity Kit for Teachers and Students of All Faiths, All Backgrounds

Additional activity sheets available:

8-Student Activity Sheet Pack (40 sheets/5 sessions), ISBN 1-58023-058-X **$19.95**

Single-Student Activity Sheet Pack (5 sessions), ISBN 1-58023-059-8 **$3.95**

In God's Name

Like an ancient myth in its poetic text and vibrant illustrations, this award-winning modern fable about the search for God's name celebrates the diversity and, at the same time, the unity of all people.

9 x 12, 32 pp, Full-color illus., Hardcover, ISBN 1-879045-26-5 **$16.99** *For ages 4 & up*

Also Available as a Board Book: **What Is God's Name?**

5 x 5, 24 pp, Board, Full-color illus., ISBN 1-893361-10-1 **$7.99** *For ages 0–4 (A SkyLight Paths book)*

Also Available: **In God's Name video and study guide**

Computer animation, original music, and children's voices. 18 min. **$29.99**

Also Available in Spanish: **El nombre de Dios**

9 x 12, 32 pp, Full-color illus., Hardcover, ISBN 1-893361-63-2 **$16.95** *(A SkyLight Paths book)*

Noah's Wife: The Story of Naamah

When God tells Noah to bring the animals of the world onto the ark, God also calls on Naamah, Noah's wife, to save each plant on Earth. Based on an ancient text.

9 x 12, 32 pp, Full-color illus., Hardcover, ISBN 1-58023-134-9 **$16.95** *For ages 4 & up*

Also Available as a Board Book: **Naamah, Noah's Wife**

5 x 5, 24 pp, Full-color illus., Board, ISBN 1-893361-56-X **$7.95** *For ages 0–4 (A SkyLight Paths book)*

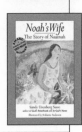

For Heaven's Sake: Finding God in Unexpected Places

9 x 12, 32 pp, Full-color illus., Hardcover, ISBN 1-58023-054-7 **$16.95** *For ages 4 & up*

God Said Amen: Finding the Answers to Our Prayers

9 x 12, 32 pp, Full-color illus., Hardcover, ISBN 1-58023-080-6 **$16.95** *For ages 4 & up*

Inspiration

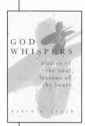

God in All Moments
Mystical & Practical Spiritual Wisdom from Hasidic Masters
Edited and translated by Or N. Rose with Ebn D. Leader
Hasidic teachings on how to be mindful in religious practice and cultivating everyday ethical behavior—*hanhagot.* 5½ x 8½, 192 pp, Quality PB, ISBN 1-58023-186-1 **$16.95**

Our Dance with God: Finding Prayer, Perspective and Meaning in the Stories of Our Lives *By Karyn D. Kedar*
Inspiring spiritual insight to guide you on your life journeys and teach you to live and thrive in two conflicting worlds: the rational/material and the spiritual.
6 x 9, 176 pp, Quality PB, ISBN 1-58023-202-7 **$16.99**

Also Available: **The Dance of the Dolphin** (Hardcover edition of *Our Dance with God*)
6 x 9, 176 pp, Hardcover, ISBN 1-58023-154-3 **$19.95**

The Empty Chair: Finding Hope and Joy—Timeless Wisdom from a Hasidic Master, Rebbe Nachman of Breslov *Adapted by Moshe Mykoff and the Breslov Research Institute*
4 x 6, 128 pp, 2-color text, Deluxe PB w/flaps, ISBN 1-879045-67-2 **$9.95**

The Gentle Weapon: Prayers for Everyday and Not-So-Everyday Moments—
Timeless Wisdom from the Teachings of the Hasidic Master, Rebbe Nachman of Breslov
Adapted by Moshe Mykoff and S. C. Mizrahi, together with the Breslov Research Institute
4 x 6, 144 pp, 2-color text, Deluxe PB w/flaps, ISBN 1-58023-022-9 **$9.99**

God Whispers: Stories of the Soul, Lessons of the Heart *By Karyn D. Kedar*
6 x 9, 176 pp, Quality PB, ISBN 1-58023-088-1 **$15.95**

An Orphan in History: One Man's Triumphant Search for His Jewish Roots
By Paul Cowan. Afterword by Rachel Cowan. 6 x 9, 288 pp, Quality PB, ISBN 1-58023-135-7 **$16.95**

Restful Reflections: Nighttime Inspiration to Calm the Soul, Based on Jewish Wisdom
By Rabbi Kerry M. Olitzky & Rabbi Lori Forman 4½ x 6½, 448 pp, Quality PB, ISBN 1-58023-091-1 **$15.95**

Sacred Intentions: Daily Inspiration to Strengthen the Spirit, Based on Jewish Wisdom
By Rabbi Kerry M. Olitzky and Rabbi Lori Forman 4½ x 6½, 448 pp, Quality PB, ISBN 1-58023-061-X **$15.95**

Kabbalah/Mysticism/Enneagram

Awakening to Kabbalah: The Guiding Light of Spiritual Fulfillment
By Rav Michael Laitman, PhD
A distinctive, personal and awe-filled introduction to this ancient wisdom tradition.
6 x 9, 192 pp, Hardcover, ISBN 1-58023-264-7 **$21.99**

Seek My Face: A Jewish Mystical Theology
By Dr. Arthur Green
This classic work of contemporary Jewish theology, revised and updated, is a profound, deeply personal statement of the lasting truths of Jewish mysticism and the basic faith claims of Judaism. 6 x 9, 304 pp, Quality PB, ISBN 1-58023-130-6 **$19.95**

Zohar: Annotated & Explained
Translation and annotation by Dr. Daniel C. Matt. Foreword by Andrew Harvey
Offers insightful yet unobtrusive commentary to the masterpiece of Jewish mysticism. 5½ x 8½, 160 pp, Quality PB, ISBN 1-893361-51-9 **$15.99** *(A SkyLight Paths book)*

Cast in God's Image: Discover Your Personality Type Using the Enneagram and Kabbalah
By Rabbi Howard A. Addison
7 x 9, 176 pp, Quality PB, Layflat binding, 20+ journaling exercises, ISBN 1-58023-124-1 **$16.95**

Ehyeh: A Kabbalah for Tomorrow *By Dr. Arthur Green*
6 x 9, 224 pp, Quality PB, ISBN 1-58023-213-2 **$16.99;** Hardcover, ISBN 1-58023-125-X **$21.95**

The Enneagram and Kabbalah, 2nd Edition: Reading Your Soul
By Rabbi Howard A. Addison 6 x 9, 192 pp, Quality PB, ISBN 1-58023-229-9 **$16.99**

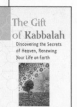

Finding Joy: A Practical Spiritual Guide to Happiness *By Dannel I. Schwartz with Mark Hass*
6 x 9, 192 pp, Quality PB, ISBN 1-58023-009-1 **$14.95**

The Gift of Kabbalah: Discovering the Secrets of Heaven, Renewing Your Life on Earth
By Tamar Frankiel, PhD
6 x 9, 256 pp, Quality PB, ISBN 1-58023-141-1 **$16.95;** Hardcover, ISBN 1-58023-108-X **$21.95**

The Way Into Jewish Mystical Tradition *By Lawrence Kushner*
6 x 9, 224 pp, Quality PB, ISBN 1-58023-200-0 **$18.99;** Hardcover, ISBN 1-58023-029-6 **$21.95**

Current Events/History

The Story of the Jews: A 4,000-Year Adventure—A Graphic History Book
Written & illustrated by Stan Mack
Witty, illustrated narrative of all the major happenings from biblical times to the twenty-first century. 6 x 9, 288 pp., illus., Quality PB, ISBN 1-58023-155-1 **$16.95**

Hannah Senesh: Her Life and Diary, the First Complete Edition
By Hannah Senesh; Foreword by Marge Piercy; Preface by Eitan Senesh
6 x 9, 352 pp, Hardcover, ISBN 1-58023-212-4 **$24.99**

The Jewish Prophet: Visionary Words from Moses and Miriam to Henrietta Szold and A. J. Heschel *By Rabbi Michael J. Shire*
6½ x 8½, 128 pp, 123 full-color illus., Hardcover, ISBN 1-58023-168-3 **Special gift price $14.95**

Shared Dreams: Martin Luther King, Jr. & the Jewish Community
By Rabbi Marc Schneier. Preface by Martin Luther King III.
6 x 9, 240 pp, Hardcover, ISBN 1-58023-062-8 **$24.95**

"Who Is a Jew?": Conversations, Not Conclusions *By Meryl Hyman*
6 x 9, 272 pp, Quality PB, ISBN 1-58023-052-0 **$16.95**

Ecology

Ecology & the Jewish Spirit: Where Nature & the Sacred Meet
Edited by Ellen Bernstein 6 x 9, 288 pp, Quality PB, ISBN 1-58023-082-2 **$16.95**

Torah of the Earth: Exploring 4,000 Years of Ecology in Jewish Thought
Vol. 1: Biblical Israel: One Land, One People; Rabbinic Judaism: One People, Many Lands
Vol. 2: Zionism: One Land, Two Peoples; Eco-Judaism: One Earth, Many Peoples
Edited by Rabbi Arthur Waskow
Vol. 1: 6 x 9, 272 pp, Quality PB, ISBN 1-58023-086-5 **$19.95**
Vol. 2: 6 x 9, 336 pp, Quality PB, ISBN 1-58023-087-3 **$19.95**

The Way Into Judaism and the Environment
By Jeremy Benstein, PhD
6 x 9, 225 pp (est.), Hardcover, ISBN 1-58023-268-X **$24.99**

Grief/Healing

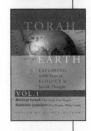

Against the Dying of the Light: A Parent's Story of Love, Loss and Hope
By Leonard Fein
5½ x 8½, 176 pp, Quality PB, ISBN 1-58023-197-7 **$15.99;** Hardcover, ISBN 1-58023-110-1 **$19.95**

Grief in Our Seasons: A Mourner's Kaddish Companion *By Rabbi Kerry M. Olitzky*
4½ x 6½, 448 pp, Quality PB, ISBN 1-879045-55-9 **$15.95**

Healing of Soul, Healing of Body: Spiritual Leaders Unfold the Strength & Solace in Psalms *Edited by Rabbi Simkha Y. Weintraub, C.S.W.*
6 x 9, 128 pp, 2-color illus. text, Quality PB, ISBN 1-879045-31-1 **$14.99**

Jewish Paths toward Healing and Wholeness: A Personal Guide to Dealing with Suffering *By Rabbi Kerry M. Olitzky. Foreword by Debbie Friedman.*
6 x 9, 192 pp, Quality PB, ISBN 1-58023-068-7 **$15.95**

Mourning & Mitzvah, 2nd Edition: A Guided Journal for Walking the Mourner's Path through Grief to Healing *By Anne Brener, L.C.S.W.*
7½ x 9, 304 pp, Quality PB, ISBN 1-58023-113-6 **$19.95**

The Perfect Stranger's Guide to Funerals and Grieving Practices
A Guide to Etiquette in Other People's Religious Ceremonies *Edited by Stuart M. Matlins*
6 x 9, 240 pp, Quality PB, ISBN 1-893361-20-9 **$16.95** *(A SkyLight Paths book)*

Tears of Sorrow, Seeds of Hope: A Jewish Spiritual Companion for Infertility and Pregnancy Loss *By Rabbi Nina Beth Cardin*
6 x 9, 192 pp, Hardcover, ISBN 1-58023-017-2 **$19.95**

A Time to Mourn, A Time to Comfort, 2nd Edition: A Guide to Jewish Bereavement and Comfort *By Dr. Ron Wolfson*
7 x 9, 336 pp, Quality PB, ISBN 1-58023-253-1 **$19.99**

When a Grandparent Dies: A Kid's Own Remembering Workbook for Dealing with Shiva and the Year Beyond *By Nechama Liss-Levinson, PhD*
8 x 10, 48 pp, 2-color text, Hardcover, ISBN 1-879045-44-3 **$15.95** *For ages 7–13*

Holidays/Holy Days

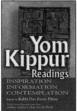

Yom Kippur Readings: Inspiration, Information and Contemplation
Edited by Rabbi Dov Peretz Elkins with section introductions from Arthur Green's These Are the Words
An extraordinary collection of readings, prayers and insights that enable the modern worshiper to enter into the spirit of the Day of Atonement in a personal and powerful way, permitting the meaning of Yom Kippur to enter the heart.
6 x 9, 348 pp, Hardcover, ISBN 1-58023-271-X **$24.99**

Leading the Passover Journey
The Seder's Meaning Revealed, the Haggadah's Story Retold
By Rabbi Nathan Laufer
Uncovers the hidden meaning of the Seder's rituals and customs.
6 x 9, 208 pp, Hardcover, ISBN 1-58023-211-6 **$24.99**

Reclaiming Judaism as a Spiritual Practice: Holy Days and Shabbat
By Rabbi Goldie Milgram
Provides a framework for understanding the powerful and often unexplained intellectual, emotional, and spiritual tools that are essential for a lively, relevant, and fulfilling Jewish spiritual practice. 7 x 9, 272 pp, Quality PB, ISBN 1-58023-205-1 **$19.99**

7th Heaven: Celebrating Shabbat with Rebbe Nachman of Breslov
By Moshe Mykoff with the Breslov Research Institute
Explores the art of consciously observing Shabbat and understanding in-depth many of the day's spiritual practices. 5⅛ x 8¼, 224 pp, Deluxe PB w/flaps, ISBN 1-58023-175-6 **$18.95**

The Women's Passover Companion
Women's Reflections on the Festival of Freedom
Edited by Rabbi Sharon Cohen Anisfeld, Tara Mohr, and Catherine Spector
Groundbreaking. A provocative conversation about women's relationships to Passover as well as the roots and meanings of women's seders.
6 x 9, 352 pp, Quality PB, ISBN 1-58023-231-0 **$19.99**; Hardcover, ISBN 1-58023-128-4 **$24.95**

The Women's Seder Sourcebook
Rituals & Readings for Use at the Passover Seder
Edited by Rabbi Sharon Cohen Anisfeld, Tara Mohr, and Catherine Spector
Gathers the voices of more than one hundred women in readings, personal and creative reflections, commentaries, blessings, and ritual suggestions that can be incorporated into your Passover celebration.
6 x 9, 384 pp, Quality PB, ISBN 1-58023-232-9 **$19.99**; Hardcover, ISBN 1-58023-136-5 **$24.95**

Creating Lively Passover Seders: A Sourcebook of Engaging Tales, Texts & Activities
By David Arnow, PhD 7 x 9, 416 pp, Quality PB, ISBN 1-58023-184-5 **$24.99**

Hanukkah, 2nd Edition: The Family Guide to Spiritual Celebration
By Dr. Ron Wolfson. Edited by Joel Lurie Grishaver.
7 x 9, 240 pp, illus., Quality PB, ISBN 1-58023-122-5 **$18.95**

The Jewish Family Fun Book: Holiday Projects, Everyday Activities, and Travel Ideas
with Jewish Themes *By Danielle Dardashti and Roni Sarig. Illus. by Avi Katz.*
6 x 9, 288 pp, 70+ illus. & diagrams, Quality PB, ISBN 1-58023-171-3 **$18.95**

The Jewish Gardening Cookbook: Growing Plants & Cooking for
Holidays & Festivals *By Michael Brown* 6 x 9, 224 pp, 30+ illus., Quality PB, ISBN 1-58023-116-0 **$16.95**

The Jewish Lights Book of Fun Classroom Activities: Simple and Seasonal
Projects for Teachers and Students *By Danielle Dardashti and Roni Sarig*
6 x 9, 240 pp, Quality PB, ISBN 1-58023-206-X **$19.99**

Passover, 2nd Edition: The Family Guide to Spiritual Celebration
By Dr. Ron Wolfson with Joel Lurie Grishaver 7 x 9, 352 pp, Quality PB, ISBN 1-58023-174-8 **$19.95**

Shabbat, 2nd Edition: The Family Guide to Preparing for and Celebrating the Sabbath
By Dr. Ron Wolfson 7 x 9, 320 pp, illus., Quality PB, ISBN 1-58023-164-0 **$19.95**

Sharing Blessings: Children's Stories for Exploring the Spirit of the Jewish Holidays
By Rahel Musleah and Michael Klayman
8½ x 11, 64 pp, Full-color illus., Hardcover, ISBN 1-879045-71-0 **$18.95** *For ages 6 & up*

Life Cycle
Marriage / Parenting / Family / Aging

Jewish Fathers: A Legacy of Love
Photographs by Lloyd Wolf. Essays by Paula Wolfson. Foreword by Harold S. Kushner.
Honors the role of contemporary Jewish fathers in America. Each father tells in his own words what it means to be a parent and Jewish, and what he learned from his own father. Insightful photos. 9½ x 9⅞, 144 pp with 100+ duotone photos, Hardcover, ISBN 1-58023-204-3 **$30.00**

The New Jewish Baby Album: Creating and Celebrating the Beginning of a Spiritual Life—A Jewish Lights Companion
By the Editors at Jewish Lights. Foreword by Anita Diamant. Preface by Sandy Eisenberg Sasso.
A spiritual keepsake that will be treasured for generations. More than just a memory book, *shows you how—and why it's important*—to create a Jewish home and a Jewish life. 8 x 10, 64 pp, Deluxe Padded Hardcover, Full-color illus., ISBN 1-58023-138-1 **$19.95**

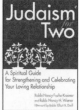

The Jewish Pregnancy Book: A Resource for the Soul, Body & Mind during Pregnancy, Birth & the First Three Months
By Sandy Falk, MD, and Rabbi Daniel Judson, with Steven A. Rapp
Includes medical information, prayers and rituals for each stage of pregnancy, from a liberal Jewish perspective. 7 x 10, 208 pp, Quality PB, b/w illus., ISBN 1-58023-178-0 **$16.95**

Celebrating Your New Jewish Daughter: Creating Jewish Ways to Welcome Baby Girls into the Covenant—New and Traditional Ceremonies
By Debra Nussbaum Cohen 6 x 9, 272 pp, Quality PB, ISBN 1-58023-090-3 **$18.95**

The New Jewish Baby Book, 2nd Edition: Names, Ceremonies & Customs—A Guide for Today's Families *By Anita Diamant* 6 x 9, 336 pp, Quality PB, ISBN 1-58023-251-5 **$19.99**

Parenting As a Spiritual Journey: Deepening Ordinary and Extraordinary Events into Sacred Occasions *By Rabbi Nancy Fuchs-Kreimer* 6 x 9, 224 pp, Quality PB, ISBN 1-58023-016-4 **$16.95**

Judaism for Two: A Spiritual Guide for Strengthening and Celebrating Your Loving Relationship *By Rabbi Nancy Fuchs-Kreimer and Rabbi Nancy H. Wiener*
Addresses the ways Jewish teachings can enhance and strengthen committed relationships. 6 x 9, 208 pp, Quality PB, ISBN 1-58023-254-X **$16.99**

Embracing the Covenant: Converts to Judaism Talk About Why & How
By Rabbi Allan Berkowitz and Patti Moskovitz 6 x 9, 192 pp, Quality PB, ISBN 1-879045-50-8 **$16.95**

The Guide to Jewish Interfaith Family Life: An InterfaithFamily.com Handbook
Edited by Ronnie Friedland and Edmund Case 6 x 9, 384 pp, Quality PB, ISBN 1-58023-153-5 **$18.95**

Introducing My Faith and My Community
The Jewish Outreach Institute Guide for the Christian in a Jewish Interfaith Relationship
By Rabbi Kerry M. Olitzky 6 x 9, 176 pp, Quality PB, ISBN 1-58023-192-6 **$16.99**

Making a Successful Jewish Interfaith Marriage: The Jewish Outreach Institute Guide to Opportunities, Challenges and Resources
By Rabbi Kerry M. Olitzky with Joan Peterson Littman 6 x 9, 176 pp, Quality PB, ISBN 1-58023-170-5 **$16.95**

The Creative Jewish Wedding Book: A Hands-On Guide to New & Old Traditions, Ceremonies & Celebrations *By Gabrielle Kaplan-Mayer*
Provides the tools to create the most meaningful Jewish traditional or alternative wedding by using ritual elements to express your unique style and spirituality. 9 x 9, 288 pp, b/w photos, Quality PB, ISBN 1-58023-194-2 **$19.99**

Divorce Is a Mitzvah: A Practical Guide to Finding Wholeness and Holiness When Your Marriage Dies *By Rabbi Perry Netter. Afterword by Rabbi Laura Geller.*
6 x 9, 224 pp, Quality PB, ISBN 1-58023-172-1 **$16.95**

A Heart of Wisdom: Making the Jewish Journey from Midlife through the Elder Years
Edited by Susan Berrin. Foreword by Harold Kushner. 6 x 9, 384 pp, Quality PB, ISBN 1-58023-051-2 **$18.95**

So That Your Values Live On: Ethical Wills and How to Prepare Them
Edited by Jack Riemer and Nathaniel Stampfer 6 x 9, 272 pp, Quality PB, ISBN 1-879045-34-6 **$18.99**

Meditation

The Handbook of Jewish Meditation Practices
A Guide for Enriching the Sabbath and Other Days of Your Life
By Rabbi David A. Cooper
Easy-to-learn meditation techniques. 6 x 9, 208 pp, Quality PB, ISBN 1-58023-102-0 **$16.95**

Discovering Jewish Meditation: Instruction & Guidance for Learning an Ancient
Spiritual Practice *By Nan Fink Gefen, PhD* 6 x 9, 208 pp, Quality PB, ISBN 1-58023-067-9 **$16.95**

A Heart of Stillness: A Complete Guide to Learning the Art of Meditation
By Rabbi David A. Cooper 5½ x 8½, 272 pp, Quality PB, ISBN 1-893361-03-9 **$16.95**
(A SkyLight Paths book)

Meditation from the Heart of Judaism: Today's Teachers Share Their
Practices, Techniques, and Faith *Edited by Avram Davis*
6 x 9, 256 pp, Quality PB, ISBN 1-58023-049-0 **$16.95**

Silence, Simplicity & Solitude: A Complete Guide to Spiritual Retreat at Home
By Rabbi David A. Cooper 5½ x 8½, 336 pp, Quality PB, ISBN 1-893361-04-7 **$16.95**
(A SkyLight Paths book)

The Way of Flame: A Guide to the Forgotten Mystical Tradition of Jewish
Meditation *By Avram Davis* 4½ x 8, 176 pp, Quality PB, ISBN 1-58023-060-1 **$15.95**

Ritual/Sacred Practice/Journaling

The Jewish Dream Book: The Key to Opening the Inner Meaning of
Your Dreams *By Vanessa L. Ochs with Elizabeth Ochs; Full-color illus. by Kristina Swarner*
Instructions for how modern people can perform ancient Jewish dream practices
and dream interpretations drawn from the Jewish wisdom tradition. For anyone
who wants to understand their dreams—and themselves.
8 x 8, 120 pp, Full-color illus., Deluxe PB w/flaps, ISBN 1-58023-132-2 **$16.95**

The Jewish Journaling Book: How to Use Jewish Tradition to Write
Your Life & Explore Your Soul *By Janet Ruth Falon*
Details the history of Jewish journaling throughout biblical and modern times,
and teaches specific journaling techniques to help you create and maintain a vital
journal, from a Jewish perspective. 8 x 8, 304 pp, Deluxe PB w/flaps, ISBN 1-58023-203-5 **$18.99**

The Book of Jewish Sacred Practices: CLAL's Guide to Everyday & Holiday
Rituals & Blessings *Edited by Rabbi Irwin Kula and Vanessa L. Ochs, PhD*
6 x 9, 368 pp, Quality PB, ISBN 1-58023-152-7 **$18.95**

Jewish Ritual: A Brief Introduction for Christians
By Rabbi Kerry M. Olitzky and Rabbi Daniel Judson
5½ x 8½, 144 pp, Quality PB, ISBN 1-58023-210-8 **$14.99**

The Rituals & Practices of a Jewish Life: A Handbook for Personal Spiritual
Renewal *Edited by Rabbi Kerry M. Olitzky and Rabbi Daniel Judson*
6 x 9, 272 pp, illus., Quality PB, ISBN 1-58023-169-1 **$18.95**

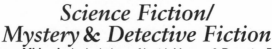

Science Fiction/ Mystery & Detective Fiction

Mystery Midrash: An Anthology of Jewish Mystery & Detective Fiction
Edited by Lawrence W. Raphael. Preface by Joel Siegel.
6 x 9, 304 pp, Quality PB, ISBN 1-58023-055-5 **$16.95**

Criminal Kabbalah: An Intriguing Anthology of Jewish Mystery & Detective Fiction
Edited by Lawrence W. Raphael. Foreword by Laurie R. King.
6 x 9, 256 pp, Quality PB, ISBN 1-58023-109-8 **$16.95**

Wandering Stars: An Anthology of Jewish Fantasy & Science Fiction
Edited by Jack Dann. Introduction by Isaac Asimov.
6 x 9, 272 pp, Quality PB, ISBN 1-58023-005-9 **$16.95**

More Wandering Stars: An Anthology of Outstanding Stories of Jewish Fantasy and
Science Fiction *Edited by Jack Dann. Introduction by Isaac Asimov.*
6 x 9, 192 pp, Quality PB, ISBN 1-58023-063-6 **$16.95**

Spirituality

Does the Soul Survive? A Jewish Journey to Belief in Afterlife, Past
Lives & Living with Purpose *By Rabbi Elie Kaplan Spitz. Foreword by Brian L. Weiss, MD*
Spitz relates his own experiences and those shared with him by people he has
worked with as a rabbi, and shows us that belief in afterlife and past lives, so
often approached with reluctance, is in fact true to Jewish tradition.
6 x 9, 288 pp, Quality PB, ISBN 1-58023-165-9 **$16.99**; Hardcover, ISBN 1-58023-094-6 **$21.95**

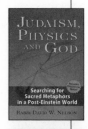

First Steps to a New Jewish Spirit: Reb Zalman's Guide to
Recapturing the Intimacy & Ecstasy in Your Relationship with God
By Rabbi Zalman M. Schachter-Shalomi with Donald Gropman
An extraordinary spiritual handbook that restores psychic and physical vigor by
introducing us to new models and alternative ways of practicing Judaism. Offers
meditation and contemplation exercises for enriching the most important aspects
of everyday life. 6 x 9, 144 pp, Quality PB, ISBN 1-58023-182-9 **$16.95**

God in Our Relationships: Spirituality between People from the
Teachings of Martin Buber *By Rabbi Dennis S. Ross*
On the eightieth anniversary of Buber's classic work, we can discover new
answers to critical issues in our lives. Inspiring examples from Ross's own life—
as congregational rabbi, father, hospital chaplain, social worker, and husband—
illustrate Buber's difficult-to-understand ideas about how we encounter God and
each other. 5½ x 8½, 160 pp, Quality PB, ISBN 1-58023-147-0 **$16.95**

Judaism, Physics and God: Searching for Sacred Metaphors in
a Post-Einstein World *By Rabbi David W. Nelson*
In clear, non-technical terms, this provocative fusion of religion and science
examines the great theories of modern physics to find new ways for contemporary people to express their spiritual beliefs and thoughts.
6 x 9, 352 pp, Quality PB, ISBN 1-58023-306-6 **$18.99**; Hardcover, ISBN 1-58023-252-3 **$24.99**

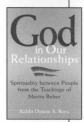

The Jewish Lights Spirituality Handbook: A Guide to Understanding,
Exploring & Living a Spiritual Life *Edited by Stuart M. Matlins*
What exactly is "Jewish" about spirituality? How do I make it a part of my life?
Fifty of today's foremost spiritual leaders share their ideas and experience with us.
6 x 9, 456 pp, Quality PB, ISBN 1-58023-093-8 **$19.95**; Hardcover, ISBN 1-58023-100-4 **$24.95**

Bringing the Psalms to Life: How to Understand and Use the Book of Psalms
By Dr. Daniel F. Polish
6 x 9, 208 pp, Quality PB, ISBN 1-58023-157-8 **$16.95**; Hardcover, ISBN 1-58023-077-6 **$21.95**

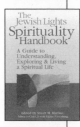

God & the Big Bang: Discovering Harmony between Science & Spirituality
By Dr. Daniel C. Matt 6 x 9, 216 pp, Quality PB, ISBN 1-879045-89-3 **$16.99**

Godwrestling—Round 2: Ancient Wisdom, Future Paths
By Rabbi Arthur Waskow 6 x 9, 352 pp, Quality PB, ISBN 1-879045-72-9 **$18.95**

One God Clapping: The Spiritual Path of a Zen Rabbi *By Rabbi Alan Lew with Sherril Jaffe*
5½ x 8½, 336 pp, Quality PB, ISBN 1-58023-115-2 **$16.95**

The Path of Blessing: Experiencing the Energy and Abundance of the Divine
By Rabbi Marcia Prager 5½ x 8½, 240 pp, Quality PB, ISBN 1-58023-148-9 **$16.95**

Six Jewish Spiritual Paths: A Rationalist Looks at Spirituality *By Rabbi Rifat Sonsino*
6 x 9, 208 pp, Quality PB, ISBN 1-58023-167-5 **$16.95**; Hardcover, ISBN 1-58023-095-4 **$21.95**

Soul Judaism: Dancing with God into a New Era
By Rabbi Wayne Dosick 5½ x 8½, 304 pp, Quality PB, ISBN 1-58023-053-9 **$16.95**

Stepping Stones to Jewish Spiritual Living: Walking the Path Morning, Noon,
and Night *By Rabbi James L. Mirel and Karen Bonnell Werth*
6 x 9, 240 pp, Quality PB, ISBN 1-58023-074-1 **$16.95**; Hardcover, ISBN 1-58023-003-2 **$21.95**

There Is No Messiah ... and You're It: The Stunning Transformation of Judaism's
Most Provocative Idea *By Rabbi Robert N. Levine, DD*
6 x 9, 192 pp, Quality PB, ISBN 1-58023-255-8 **$16.99**; Hardcover, ISBN 1-58023-173-X **$21.95**

These Are the Words: A Vocabulary of Jewish Spiritual Life *By Dr. Arthur Green*
6 x 9, 304 pp, Quality PB, ISBN 1-58023-107-1 **$18.95**

Spirituality/Women's Interest

The Quotable Jewish Woman: Wisdom, Inspiration & Humor from the Mind & Heart *Edited and compiled by Elaine Bernstein Partnow*
The definitive collection of ideas, reflections, humor, and wit of over 300 Jewish women.
6 x 9, 496 pp, Hardcover, ISBN 1-58023-193-4 **$29.99**

Lifecycles, Vol. 1: Jewish Women on Life Passages & Personal Milestones
Edited and with introductions by Rabbi Debra Orenstein 6 x 9, 480 pp, Quality PB, ISBN 1-58023-018-0 **$19.95**
Lifecycles, Vol. 2: Jewish Women on Biblical Themes in Contemporary Life
Edited and with introductions by Rabbi Debra Orenstein and Rabbi Jane Rachel Litman
6 x 9, 464 pp, Quality PB, ISBN 1-58023-019-9 **$19.95**
Moonbeams: A Hadassah Rosh Hodesh Guide *Edited by Carol Diament, PhD*
8½ x 11, 240 pp, Quality PB, ISBN 1-58023-099-7 **$20.00**

ReVisions: Seeing Torah through a Feminist Lens *By Rabbi Elyse Goldstein*
5½ x 8½, 224 pp, Quality PB, ISBN 1-58023-117-9 **$16.95**
White Fire: A Portrait of Women Spiritual Leaders in America
By Rabbi Malka Drucker. Photographs by Gay Block.
7 x 10, 320 pp, 30+ b/w photos, Hardcover, ISBN 1-893361-64-0 **$24.95** *(A SkyLight Paths book)*
Women of the Wall: Claiming Sacred Ground at Judaism's Holy Site
Edited by Phyllis Chesler and Rivka Haut 6 x 9, 496 pp, b/w photos, Hardcover, ISBN 1-58023-161-6 **$34.95**
The Women's Haftarah Commentary: New Insights from Women Rabbis on the 54 Weekly Haftarah Portions, the 5 Megillot & Special Shabbatot
Edited by Rabbi Elyse Goldstein 6 x 9, 560 pp, Hardcover, ISBN 1-58023-133-0 **$39.99**
The Women's Torah Commentary: New Insights from Women Rabbis on the 54 Weekly Torah Portions *Edited by Rabbi Elyse Goldstein*
6 x 9, 496 pp, Hardcover, ISBN 1-58023-076-8 **$34.95**
The Year Mom Got Religion: One Woman's Midlife Journey into Judaism
By Lee Meyerhoff Hendler 6 x 9, 208 pp, Quality PB, ISBN 1-58023-070-9 **$15.95**

See Holidays for *The Women's Passover Companion: Women's Reflections on the Festival of Freedom* and *The Women's Seder Sourcebook: Rituals & Readings for Use at the Passover Seder.* Also see Bar/Bat Mitzvah for *The JGirl's Guide: The Young Jewish Woman's Handbook for Coming of Age.*

Travel

Israel—A Spiritual Travel Guide, 2nd Edition
A Companion for the Modern Jewish Pilgrim
By Rabbi Lawrence A. Hoffman 4¼ x 10, 256 pp, Quality PB, illus., ISBN 1-58023-261-2 **$18.99**
Also Available: **The Israel Mission Leader's Guide** ISBN 1-58023-085-7 **$4.95**

12 Steps

100 Blessings Every Day Daily Twelve Step Recovery Affirmations, Exercises for Personal Growth & Renewal Reflecting Seasons of the Jewish Year
By Rabbi Kerry M. Olitzky. Foreword by Rabbi Neil Gillman.
One-day-at-a-time monthly format. Reflects on the rhythm of the Jewish calendar to bring insight to recovery from addictions.
4½ x 6½, 432 pp, Quality PB, ISBN 1-879045-30-3 **$15.99**

Recovery from Codependence: A Jewish Twelve Steps Guide to Healing Your Soul
By Rabbi Kerry M. Olitzky 6 x 9, 160 pp, Quality PB, ISBN 1-879045-32-X **$13.95**
Renewed Each Day: Daily Twelve Step Recovery Meditations Based on the Bible
By Rabbi Kerry M. Olitzky and Aaron Z.
Vol. 1—Genesis & Exodus: 6 x 9, 224 pp, Quality PB, ISBN 1-879045-12-5 **$14.95**
Vol. 2—Leviticus, Numbers & Deuteronomy: 6 x 9, 280 pp, Quality PB, ISBN 1-879045-13-3 **$18.99**
Twelve Jewish Steps to Recovery: A Personal Guide to Turning from Alcoholism & Other Addictions—Drugs, Food, Gambling, Sex ...
By Rabbi Kerry M. Olitzky and Stuart A. Copans, MD Preface by Abraham J. Twerski, MD
6 x 9, 144 pp, Quality PB, ISBN 1-879045-09-5 **$14.95**

Spirituality/The Way Into... Series

The Way Into... Series offers an accessible and highly usable "guided tour" of the Jewish faith, people, history and beliefs—in total, an introduction to Judaism that will enable you to understand and interact with the sacred texts of the Jewish tradition. Each volume is written by a leading contemporary scholar and teacher, and explores one key aspect of Judaism. The Way Into... enables all readers to achieve a real sense of Jewish cultural literacy through guided study.

The Way Into Encountering God in Judaism By Neil Gillman
6 x 9, 240 pp, Quality PB, ISBN 1-58023-199-3 **$18.99**; Hardcover, ISBN 1-58023-025-3 **$21.95**

Also Available: **The Jewish Approach to God: A Brief Introduction for Christians**
By Neil Gillman 5½ x 8½, 192 pp, Quality PB, ISBN 1-58023-190-X **$16.95**

The Way Into Jewish Mystical Tradition By Lawrence Kushner
6 x 9, 224 pp, Quality PB, ISBN 1-58023-200-0 **$18.99**; Hardcover, ISBN 1-58023-029-6 **$21.95**

The Way Into Jewish Prayer By Lawrence A. Hoffman
6 x 9, 224 pp, Quality PB, ISBN 1-58023-201-9 **$18.99**; Hardcover, ISBN 1-58023-027-X **$21.95**

The Way Into Judaism and the Environment By Jeremy Benstein, PhD
6 x 9, 225 pp (est.), Hardcover, ISBN 1-58023-268-X **$24.99**

The Way Into Tikkun Olam (Repairing the World) By Elliot N. Dorff
6 x 9, 320 pp, Hardcover, ISBN 1-58023-269-8 **$24.99**

The Way Into Torah By Norman J. Cohen
6 x 9, 176 pp, Quality PB, ISBN 1-58023-198-5 **$16.99**; Hardcover, ISBN 1-58023-028-8 **$21.95**

Spirituality and Wellness

Aleph-Bet Yoga
Embodying the Hebrew Letters for Physical and Spiritual Well-Being
By Steven A. Rapp. Foreword by Tamar Frankiel, PhD, and Judy Greenfeld. Preface by Hart Lazer
7 x 10, 128 pp, b/w photos, Quality PB, Layflat binding, ISBN 1-58023-162-4 **$16.95**

Entering the Temple of Dreams
Jewish Prayers, Movements, and Meditations for the End of the Day
By Tamar Frankiel, PhD, and Judy Greenfeld
7 x 10, 192 pp, illus., Quality PB, ISBN 1-58023-079-2 **$16.95**

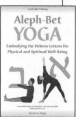

Jewish Paths toward Healing and Wholeness: A Personal Guide to Dealing
with Suffering By Rabbi Kerry M. Olitzky. Foreword by Debbie Friedman.
6 x 9, 192 pp, Quality PB, ISBN 1-58023-068-7 **$15.95**

Minding the Temple of the Soul
Balancing Body, Mind, and Spirit through Traditional Jewish Prayer, Movement, and
Meditation By Tamar Frankiel, PhD, and Judy Greenfeld
7 x 10, 184 pp, illus., Quality PB, ISBN 1-879045-64-8 **$16.95**
Audiotape of the Blessings and Meditations: 60 min. **$9.95**
Videotape of the Movements and Meditations: 46 min. **$20.00**

Spirituality/Lawrence Kushner

Filling Words with Light: Hasidic and Mystical Reflections on Jewish Prayer
By Lawrence Kushner and Nehemia Polen
Reflects on the joy, gratitude, mystery and awe embedded in traditional prayers and blessings, and shows how you can imbue these familiar sacred words with your own sense of holiness. 5½ x 8½, 176 pp, Hardcover, ISBN 1-58023-216-7 **$21.99**

The Book of Letters: A Mystical Hebrew Alphabet
Popular Hardcover Edition, 6 x 9, 80 pp, 2-color text, ISBN 1-879045-00-1 **$24.95**
Collector's Limited Edition, 9 x 12, 80 pp, gold foil embossed pages, w/limited edition silkscreened print, ISBN 1-879045-04-4 **$349.00**

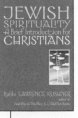

The Book of Miracles: A Young Person's Guide to Jewish Spiritual Awareness
6 x 9, 96 pp, 2-color illus., Hardcover, ISBN 1-879045-78-8 **$16.95** *For ages 9–13*

The Book of Words: Talking Spiritual Life, Living Spiritual Talk
6 x 9, 160 pp, Quality PB, ISBN 1-58023-020-2 **$16.95**

Eyes Remade for Wonder: A Lawrence Kushner Reader *Introduction by Thomas Moore*
6 x 9, 240 pp, Quality PB, ISBN 1-58023-042-3 **$18.95;** Hardcover, ISBN 1-58023-014-8 **$23.95**

God Was in This Place & I, i Did Not Know
Finding Self, Spirituality and Ultimate Meaning 6 x 9, 192 pp, Quality PB, ISBN 1-879045-33-8 **$16.95**

Honey from the Rock: An Introduction to Jewish Mysticism
6 x 9, 176 pp, Quality PB, ISBN 1-58023-073-3 **$16.95**

Invisible Lines of Connection: Sacred Stories of the Ordinary
5½ x 8½, 160 pp, Quality PB, ISBN 1-879045-98-2 **$15.95**

Jewish Spirituality—A Brief Introduction for Christians
5½ x 8½, 112 pp, Quality PB Original, ISBN 1-58023-150-0 **$12.95**

The River of Light: Jewish Mystical Awareness 6 x 9, 192 pp, Quality PB, ISBN 1-58023-096-2 **$16.95**

The Way Into Jewish Mystical Tradition
6 x 9, 224 pp, Quality PB, ISBN 1-58023-200-0 **$18.99;** Hardcover, ISBN 1-58023-029-6 **$21.95**

Spirituality/Prayer

Pray Tell: A Hadassah Guide to Jewish Prayer
By Rabbi Jules Harlow, with contributions from Tamara Cohen, Rochelle Furstenberg, Rabbi Daniel Gordis, Leora Tanenbaum, and many others
Enriched with insight and wisdom from a broad variety of viewpoints.
8½ x 11, 400 pp, Quality PB, ISBN 1-58023-163-2 **$29.95**

My People's Prayer Book Series
Traditional Prayers, Modern Commentaries *Edited by Rabbi Lawrence A. Hoffman*
Provides diverse and exciting commentary to the traditional liturgy, helping modern men and women find new wisdom in Jewish prayer, and bring liturgy into their lives. Each book includes Hebrew text, modern translation, and commentaries from all perspectives of the Jewish world.

Vol. 1—The *Sh'ma* and Its Blessings
7 x 10, 168 pp, Hardcover, ISBN 1-879045-79-6 **$24.99**
Vol. 2—The *Amidah*
7 x 10, 240 pp, Hardcover, ISBN 1-879045-80-X **$24.95**
Vol. 3—*P'sukei D'zimrah* (Morning Psalms)
7 x 10, 240 pp, Hardcover, ISBN 1-879045-81-8 **$24.95**
Vol. 4—*Seder K'riat Hatorah* (The Torah Service)
7 x 10, 264 pp, Hardcover, ISBN 1-879045-82-6 **$23.95**
Vol. 5—*Birkhot Hashachar* (Morning Blessings)
7 x 10, 240 pp, Hardcover, ISBN 1-879045-83-4 **$24.95**
Vol. 6—*Tachanun* and Concluding Prayers
7 x 10, 240 pp, Hardcover, ISBN 1-879045-84-2 **$24.95**
Vol. 7—Shabbat at Home
7 x 10, 240 pp, Hardcover, ISBN 1-879045-85-0 **$24.95**
Vol. 8—*Kabbalat Shabbat* (Welcoming Shabbat in the Synagogue)
7 x 10, 240 pp, Hardcover, ISBN 1-58023-121-7 **$24.99**
Vol. 9—Welcoming the Night: *Minchah* and *Ma'ariv* (Afternoon and Evening Prayer) 7 x 10, 272 pp, Hardcover, ISBN 1-58023-262-0 **$24.99**

Theology/Philosophy

Aspects of Rabbinic Theology
By Solomon Schechter. New Introduction by Dr. Neil Gillman.
6 x 9, 448 pp, Quality PB, ISBN 1-879045-24-9 **$19.95**

Broken Tablets: Restoring the Ten Commandments and Ourselves
Edited by Rachel S. Mikva. Introduction by Lawrence Kushner. Afterword by Arnold Jacob Wolf.
6 x 9, 192 pp, Quality PB, ISBN 1-58023-158-6 **$16.95**; Hardcover, ISBN 1-58023-066-0 **$21.95**

Creating an Ethical Jewish Life
A Practical Introduction to Classic Teachings on How to Be a Jew
By Dr. Byron L. Sherwin and Seymour J. Cohen
6 x 9, 336 pp, Quality PB, ISBN 1-58023-114-4 **$19.95**

The Death of Death: Resurrection and Immortality in Jewish Thought
By Dr. Neil Gillman 6 x 9, 336 pp, Quality PB, ISBN 1-58023-081-4 **$18.95**

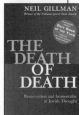

Evolving Halakhah: A Progressive Approach to Traditional Jewish Law
By Rabbi Dr. Moshe Zemer
6 x 9, 480 pp, Quality PB, ISBN 1-58023-127-6 **$29.95**; Hardcover, ISBN 1-58023-002-4 **$40.00**

Hasidic Tales: Annotated & Explained
By Rabbi Rami Shapiro. Foreword by Andrew Harvey, SkyLight Illuminations series editor.
5½ x 8½, 240 pp, Quality PB, ISBN 1-893361-86-1 **$16.95** *(A SkyLight Paths Book)*

A Heart of Many Rooms: Celebrating the Many Voices within Judaism
By Dr. David Hartman 6 x 9, 352 pp, Quality PB, ISBN 1-58023-156-X **$19.95**

The Hebrew Prophets: Selections Annotated & Explained
Translation & Annotation by Rabbi Rami Shapiro. Foreword by Zalman M. Schachter-Shalomi
5½ x 8½, 224 pp, Quality PB, ISBN 1-59473-037-7 **$16.99** *(A SkyLight Paths book)*

Keeping Faith with the Psalms: Deepen Your Relationship with God Using the
Book of Psalms *By Daniel F. Polish* 6 x 9, 320 pp, Quality PB, ISBN 1-58023-300-7 **$18.99**
Hardcover, ISBN 1-58023-179-9 **$24.95**

The Last Trial
On the Legends and Lore of the Command to Abraham to Offer Isaac as a Sacrifice
By Shalom Spiegel. New Introduction by Judah Goldin.
6 x 9, 208 pp, Quality PB, ISBN 1-879045-29-X **$18.95**

A Living Covenant: The Innovative Spirit in Traditional Judaism
By Dr. David Hartman 6 x 9, 368 pp, Quality PB, ISBN 1-58023-011-3 **$20.00**

Love and Terror in the God Encounter
The Theological Legacy of Rabbi Joseph B. Soloveitchik
By Dr. David Hartman
6 x 9, 240 pp, Quality PB, ISBN 1-58023-176-4 **$19.95**; Hardcover, ISBN 1-58023-112-8 **$25.00**

The Personhood of God: Biblical Theology, Human Faith and the Divine Image
By Dr. Yochanan Muffs; Foreword by Dr. David Hartman
6 x 9, 240 pp, Hardcover, ISBN 1-58023-265-5 **$24.99**

The Spirit of Renewal: Finding Faith after the Holocaust
By Rabbi Edward Feld 6 x 9, 224 pp, Quality PB, ISBN 1-879045-40-0 **$16.95**

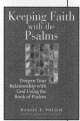

Tormented Master: *The Life and Spiritual Quest of Rabbi Nahman of Bratslav*
By Dr. Arthur Green 6 x 9, 416 pp, Quality PB, ISBN 1-879045-11-7 **$19.99**

Your Word Is Fire: The Hasidic Masters on Contemplative Prayer
Edited and translated by Dr. Arthur Green and Barry W. Holtz
6 x 9, 160 pp, Quality PB, ISBN 1-879045-25-7 **$15.95**

I Am Jewish
Personal Reflections Inspired by the Last Words of Daniel Pearl
Almost 150 Jews—both famous and not—from all walks of life, from all around
the world, write about Identity, Heritage, Covenant / Chosenness and Faith,
Humanity and Ethnicity, and *Tikkun Olam* and Justice.
Edited by Judea and Ruth Pearl
6 x 9, 304 pp, Deluxe PB w/flaps, ISBN 1-58023-259-0 **$18.99**; Hardcover, ISBN 1-58023-183-7 **$24.99**
Download a free copy of the *I Am Jewish Teacher's Guide* at our website:
www.jewishlights.com

About Jewish Lights

People of all faiths and backgrounds yearn for books that attract, engage, educate, and spiritually inspire.

Our principal goal is to stimulate thought and help all people learn about who the Jewish People are, where they come from, and what the future can be made to hold. While people of our diverse Jewish heritage are the primary audience, our books speak to people in the Christian world as well and will broaden their understanding of Judaism and the roots of their own faith.

We bring to you authors who are at the forefront of spiritual thought and experience. While each has something different to say, they all say it in a voice that you can hear.

Our books are designed to welcome you and then to engage, stimulate, and inspire. We judge our success not only by whether or not our books are beautiful and commercially successful, but by whether or not they make a difference in your life.

For your information and convenience, at the back of this book we have provided a list of other Jewish Lights books you might find interesting and useful. They cover all the categories of your life:

Bar/Bat Mitzvah	Life Cycle
Bible Study / Midrash	Meditation
Children's Books	Parenting
Congregation Resources	Prayer
Current Events / History	Ritual / Sacred Practice
Ecology	Spirituality
Fiction: Mystery, Science Fiction	Theology / Philosophy
Grief / Healing	Travel
Holidays / Holy Days	Twelve Steps
Inspiration	Women's Interest
Kabbalah / Mysticism / Enneagram	

Stuart M. Matlins, Publisher

Or phone, fax, mail or e-mail to: **JEWISH LIGHTS Publishing**
Sunset Farm Offices, Route 4 • P.O. Box 237 • Woodstock, Vermont 05091
Tel: (802) 457-4000 • Fax: (802) 457-4004 • www.jewishlights.com
Credit card orders: **(800) 962-4544** (8:30AM–5:30PM ET Monday–Friday)
Generous discounts on quantity orders. SATISFACTION GUARANTEED. Prices subject to change.

For more information about each book,
visit our website at www.jewishlights.com